Cotton Mather's
Verse in English

Cotton Mather's Verse in English

EDITED BY

Denise D. Knight

DELAWARE

Newark: University of Delaware Press
London and Toronto: Associated University Presses

Associated University Presses
440 Forsgate Drive
Cranbury, NJ 08512

Associated University Presses
25 Sicilian Avenue
London WC1A 2QH, England

Associated University Presses
P.O. Box 488, Port Credit
Mississauga, Ontario
Canada L5G 4M2

The paper used in this publication meets the requirements of the American National Standard for Permanence of Paper for Printed Library Materials Z39.48-1984.

Library of Congress Cataloging-in-Publication Data

Mather, Cotton, 1663–1728.
  Cotton Mather's verse in English / edited by Denise D. Knight.
    p.   cm.
  Bibliography: p.
  ISBN 0-87413-349-1 (alk. paper)
  1. Christian poetry, American.   I. Knight, Denise D., 1954–   .
II. Title.
RS805.A17   1989
811'.1—dc19   88-40313
                                                              CIP

PRINTED IN THE UNITED STATES OF AMERICA

Contents

Acknowledgments

I would like to express my thanks to several people and institutions for their assistance in making this project possible. I am grateful to the late Harold S. Jantz, whose book, *The First Century of New England Verse*, provided an indispensable source of information. I also owe thanks to the following for their assistance and cooperation: the American Antiquarian Society, Worcester, Massachusetts; the Brown University Library, Providence, Rhode Island; the Houghton Library, Harvard University; the Massachusetts Historical Society, Boston; the Library at the State University of New York at Albany, and the Tracey W. McGregor Library, University of Virginia.

I would also like to thank Margaret Colgate of the Classics Department at the State University of New York at Albany for her generous help in translating the numerous Latin passages. I also owe particular thanks to Professors Ronald A. Bosco, Eugene Mirabelli, and Perry Westbrook at the State University of New York at Albany for their assistance with my original draft of the text. But I am especially indebted to my husband, Michael K. Barylski, whose love, enthusiasm, and selflessness made this project possible.

Introduction

In a diary entry dated 27 September 1713, Cotton Mather recorded his distress over the contamination of spiritual purity among God's chosen people. True to his calling, Mather wasted no time in offering a cure:

> I am informed, that the Minds and Manners of many People about the Countrey are much corrupted, by foolish Songs and Ballads, which the Hawkers and Pedlars carry into all parts of the Countrey. By way of Antidote, I would procure poetical Composures full of Piety, and such as may have a Tendency to advance Truth and Goodness, to be published, and scattered into all Corners of the Land.[1]

While the passage clearly condemns the function of "foolish songs and ballads," it also elucidates Mather's view on the value of poetry: quite simply, the best, if not only, purpose of poetry is the advancement of piety, truth, and goodness.

While no real consensus has yet been reached among the critics regarding the quality or purpose of Puritan poetry as a whole, the fact that it was motivated largely by spiritual concerns is indisputable.[2] As a genre, Puritan poetry offers more variety than is generally acknowledged. It is surprisingly diverse despite its stigma of rigid piety. For instance, Indians, adultery, wildlife, storms, farming, gardening, cats, the moon, bankruptcy, and shellfish were all considered legitimate topics for poetic development. Moreover, there is a broad stylistic range in the verse, which encompasses ballads, hymns, elegies, couplets, and literal as well as liberal translations of classical and antiquarian verse. Puritan humor also manifested itself in the poetry: puns, anagrams, and satire were commonly used. Mather, however, chose to confine his poetic practice almost exclusively to the promotion of religious truths, using humor sparingly and, at that, primarily in his early verse. His desire to restrict the thematic range of his poetry had less to do with narrowness of mind (he applauded poetry from Virgil to Bradstreet) than with a haunting fear that too

11

radical a departure from his role as God's servant might attract dark spirits:

> The powers of darkness have a library among us, whereof the poets have been the most numerous as well as the most venemous authors. . . . As for those wretched scribbles of madmen, my son, touch them not, taste them not, handle them not: thou wilt perish in the using of them. . . . [T]hose vile rhapsodies . . . which you will find always leave a taint upon your mind, and among other ill effects, will sensibly indispose you to converse with the holy oracles of God your Saviour.[3]

What Mather lacked in breadth of theme he made up in range of quality. While a few of his verses come perilously close to bordering on fatuity, others are at least equal in quality to, and often better than, those of the more than two hundred early New Englanders who occasionally wrote poetry.[4] With so many people trying their hand at verse and often publishing during their lifetime, one wonders how, indeed if, Mather's verse fit into a conventional Puritan literary style. In truth, the much touted "plain style" of Puritan poets held vastly different meanings for different people.[5] Mather's occasional ventures into incredibly ornate verse defy the tradition of lucidity and brevity generally associated with the plain style. In defense of stylistic versatility, however, Mather wrote:

> [E]very man will have his own stile, which will distinguish him as much as his gait: and if you can attain to that which I have newly described, but always writing so as to give an easy conveyance unto your ideas, I would not have you by any scourging be driven out of your gait.[6]

What Mather has "newly described" is a style that "endeavours that the reader may have something to the purpose in every paragraph."[7] He blasts the "modern way of criticising," which does not provide any substantive criteria against which to judge poetical quality.[8] Not only are the critics as "contemptible" as they are "supercilious," but also "while each of them, conceitedly enough, sets up for the standard of perfection, we are entirely at a loss which fire to follow."[9] Thus, Mather's advocacy of individual style may explain in part his inclusion in his own works of others' poetry clearly more skillful in quality and diverse in subject than his own. For example, poems written by Daniel Henchman, Benjamin Thompson, and others appear in Mather's *Magnalia Christi*

12

Americana (1702). Likewise, in the massive, unpublished "Biblia Americana," Mather cites Charles Darby, Richard Blackmore, Isaac Watts, Nicholas Brady, and Nahum Tate as composing the several poems he includes. It appears, in fact, that none of the verse in the "Biblia" is of Mather's authorship.

In *Manuductio ad Ministerium*, a handbook published in 1726 for students of divinity, Mather devoted one entire chapter to the question of poetry and style. He cited the value of understanding the great epic poets and chided those who possessed no appreciation of their art:

> Though some have had a soul so unmusical, that they have decried all verse as being but a meer playing and fiddling upon words . . . I cannot wish you a soul that shall be wholly unpoetical.[10]

But Mather quickly qualified his statement, making clear that he was in no way unconditionally endorsing the virtues of poetry; on the contrary, he saw poetry as a practical method, when used properly, of expanding one's repertoire of acquired knowledge:

> [I]f you try young wings now and then to see what flights you can make, at least for an epigram, it may a little sharpen your sense, and polish your style for more important performances.[11]

The "more important performances" Mather alludes to are undoubtedly the fulfillment of ministerial obligations. Nonetheless, he draws strict limitations on the extent to which interest in poetry should be indulged:

> [Y]ou may . . . all your days make a little recreation of poetry in the midst of your painful studies. Nevertheless, I cannot but advise you . . . Be not so set upon poetry, as to be always poring on the passionate and measured pages. Let not what should be sauce, rather than food for you, engross all your application. . . . But especially preserve the chastity of your soul from the dangers you may incur, by a conversation with muses that are no better than harlots.[12]

Mather's concern about the dangers inherent in taking poetry too seriously is illustrated by his equation of muses to harlots. By recommending that the ministers make but "a little recreation of poetry," he is placing the art within what he deems to be appropriate confines. The majority of Mather's own verses, in fact, appeared not as individual works, but as appendixes, prefaces, or supplements to his nearly four hundred published works, adding

13

weight to his conviction that poetry should be viewed as "sauce" rather than "food." His eight-line epitaph on Michael Wigglesworth, for instance, seems almost perfunctory when taken out of the context of its role as a appendage to his long and highly praiseworthy sermon, *A Faithful Man, Described and Rewarded*. When viewed separately, Mather's brief allusions to Wigglesworth's famous "Day of Doom," his *Meat out of the Eater*, his frail countenance, and his following as a physician make the verse seem more like a witty conceit than a valid tribute to one of New England's more influential figures. The Wigglesworth epitaph, however, offers a good example of poetry functioning "as sauce" in conjunction with a major work.

Mather's poetry can be loosely classified into six types: religious meditations, elegies and epitaphs, verse for children, "Agricola" verse, hymns, and Bible verse. It was not unusual for his poetry to appear in various publications, sometimes with slight improvements from earlier versions. The poem occasioned on the death of Mather's wife, for example, ("Go then, my Dove") was originally produced as an epitaph, then appeared as a diary entry, and was later expanded and printed in the 1703 edition of Mather's *Meat out of the Eater*. The common denominator in all of the verse is, of course, the emphasis on religious doctrine. Unlike many of his contemporaries, Mather wrote no love poetry or domestic verse (in the tradition of Anne Bradstreet's "As loving Hind" and "In reference to her Children"), no occasional poetry or metaphysical verse (such as Edward Taylor's "Meditations"). Readers looking to Mather for a broad range of poetic themes are likely to be disappointed. Instead, his verse functioned strictly as a means to an end: it was simply an efficient way to promote the message of God. When written mnemonically, it served not only to advance religious doctrine, but also made that doctrine accessible for adults and children alike.[13] Following the lead established by the *Bay Psalm Book* and by Wigglesworth in "The Day of Doom," Mather, like many of his contemporaries, versified biblical and doctrinal precepts for easy recitation, which itself was conducive to memorization. Mather was so committed to this use of poetry that in a personally uncharacteristic break from tradition, he argued that his grandfather Richard Mather's claim that "God's Altar needs not our pollishings,"[14] was no longer pertinent to the increasingly cosmopolitan audience of late-seventeenth, early-eighteenth century New England. Instead, he argued in the *Magnalia* that the time had come to revise the *Bay Psalm Book* in a way to enhance its instructional potential. Mather answered his claim concerning the *Bay Psalm Book* ("It was thought that a little more of Art was to be employed upon the verses"[15]) with his *Psalterium Americanum*, a modern version of the psalms published in 1718.

The audience for Puritan poetry was as varied as the poetry itself.[16] Mather's readers ranged from young children to his parishioners, from family members to farmers. Intellectually, the range was wide as well, and although the bulk of his verse was intended for a general audience, one wonders whether, for instance, the typical New Englander could comprehend all the complexities and nuances that some of the elaborate elegiac verse invites.

Elegiac writing as a form of verse was highly regarded during much of Mather's lifetime, finally fading in popularity around 1720.[17] Mather's earliest poetic attempts, as far as can be documented, were, in fact, elegies. As a type of Puritan writing, the elegy had much to offer New Englanders. Employing an exhortational and a didactic tone (common sermonic devices), the elegy celebrated the life of the deceased as a model worthy of emulation for the community. At the same time, in classic elegiac fashion, New England elegies offered a consolation to survivors: the newly departed had transcended this world for a better one.

The elegy typically began with a justification as to why it was being composed. Two reasons were most often cited. First, the poem was written out of deference to the person being elegized, and second, the poet was simply following the biblical precedent of lamenting the dead in verse. The elegiac tone was serious, pious, and, above all, didactic: the death was not merely a loss to one's family and friends, but was viewed as an act of God affecting the entire community, particularly when the death of a prominent leader was perceived as a sign of God's unhappiness with his chosen people.[18] The use of anagrams and witty conceits, while straying from the much-touted plain style, was actually quite common in elegiac verse. Anagrams, the rearrangement of letters in the deceased's name, presented an occasion to discover the significance of his life, while witticisms presented merely another sophisticated means of extolling his many virtues. The elegists leaned most heavily, however, on biblical and classical allusions in espousing the virtues of their fallen heroes.

At the age of nineteen, Mather published his first major poetical work, an ambitious 429-line elegy: "A Poem Dedicated to the Memory of the Reverend and Excellent Mr. Urian Oakes."[19] That poem, written to commemorate the death of the president of Harvard College, was followed three years later by another major work in the elegiac style: "An Elegy On The Much-to-be-deplored Death of That Never-to-be forgotten Person, the Reverend Mr. Nathanael Collins."[20] In both verses, young Mather attempted to impress his audience with his command of elegiac style and purpose. In the Oakes elegy, Mather included a prefatory message to the reader, citing the historical tradition of elegiac verse as practiced not only in contemporary New England, but also in biblical times: "Worthies *to* Praise *is* a Praise-Worthy thing; Christ *did it and will do it! And to Sing The* Elogyes *of Saints departed in the* Rhythm *of* Elegyes, *has always been Esteemed* Reason!"[21] By aligning his poetic mission with that of Christ, Mather legitimized elegiac practice and granted Oakes stature akin to that of the biblical figure Jonathan.[22] Mather's enumeration of New England elegies that preceded his own served two functions: first, it lent credibility to his own practice of elegizing; second, by humbly confessing the liberty of modeling his verse after the "good examples" of those before him he freed himself from the liabilities of potential criticism:

> *I should be vain to Thrust into that gallant* Chorus. . . . *I cry'd of good* Exemples. . . . How if I should run after them? *And brought These as a* Pattern, *and a* Plea *for what I do; that my cross Reader blame me not.*[23]

Mather approached the Collins elegy in similar fashion, again alluding to the biblical precedent by citing David's lamentation of Jonathan, and then by offering a humble apology for the quality of the poem:

> *To Lament the* Dead *in* Verse, *having been even from the dayes of* David *until Now, in some sort almost as* Common *as Death itself, an* Apology *for* that *thing at this time is altogether superfluous.* . . .[24]

Mather is not apologizing for the lamentation itself; he is humbly attributing the crudeness of the elegy to his lack of experience in writing verse: "*[T]here seems more needful an Excuse for the meaness of* this *Composure, which is born before its Time from a Brain* disus'd *to such Performances.*"[25] Humble apologies are a device that surfaces often in Puritan writing, most notably for Mather in the *Magnalia*, where he cites "continual hurries" to other obligations as a factor impeding his writing.[26] In an extension of the apology, Mather compares himself to Virgil, remarking that even though he had eleven years to compose his Æneids, Virgil still felt them insufficient in quality to be published, while Mather had "[but] a *few*

16

stolen hours . . . *to shape* [the elegy] *in*."[27] Had Collins ever "given sufficient caution That his Herse should not be burdened with bad Funeral verses," Mather vowed that he would never have undertaken the task and that he expected "*no* Laurel *on this occasion but what I merit by my good Affection to the* Memory *of a* true Israelite *worthy to be* had in Everlasting Remembrance."[28]

The use of typology (the occurrence of events, patterns, and symbols present or prophesized in the Bible) is another device used by Mather, particularly in his elegies. Originating in the books of the New Testament, typological exegesis was used extensively in Puritan writings. Indeed, the application of the Old Testament prophecies and events assumed a critical role in explaining parallel experiences in the seventeenth century.[29] In a typical employment of typology, for example, Mather, in his elegy on Oakes, compares the deceased to various biblical figures: "For a Converse with God; and holy frame / *A Noah*, and an *Enoch* hee became."[30] A few lines later, Oakes is referred to as "Our *Second Moses.*"

Mather, as poet, also employs typology as he sets out to contemplate the meaning of Collins's death by comparing his spiritual journey with that of David: "into the howling *desart* thus I went." He extends the use of typology into the next several lines, discovering an *"Elect Lady,"* Collins's church at Middletown, and comparing her to the biblical Rachel, inconsolably weeping for her children. When the poet asks the church why she grieves, the church, personified, aligns herself with the widow of the Lamentations. Mather's own voice suddenly reappearing seems intrusive, but his reaffirmation of the desire not to be witty, but to pay homage to a majestic hero, serves to clarify his purpose in writing the elegy:

> Some *Elogyes* compose to try their Wits;
> The *Gout*, the *Feavour*, yea & *Injustice*,
> *Folly* and *Poverty* have in the Fits
> Of Ranting Writers had a *comeliness.*
>
> My *Theme*, my *Humour* is not such an one:
> Who to prove *Cicero* not eloquent . . .
>
> I would that you, my Friend, each *drop* of Ink
> Could fill with *Elogyes* no fewer then
> The little *eels* that may swim in't: I think
> They all should celebrate this *Flow'r of men.*

17

That Collins is worthy of emulation is unconditionally restated in the last two lines of the verse: *"Save ev'ry soul that reads this Elegy; / Like COLLINS let us live, like COLLINS dy."*[31]

Both the Oakes and Collins elegies reveal Mather's inexperienced hand with the art of poetry. Whether or not one believes the sincerity of Mather's humble apologies, they were, ironically, pretty much on target. Both early elegies are awkward and strained, stemming from clumsy analogies and the juxtaposition of obscure classical and biblical allusions that in many respects were more fitting for Mather's Harvard contemporaries than a communal New England audience. Sometimes the heavy punctuation of verse with Mather's own notes, often in Latin, becomes a source of distraction. And the random incorporation of such rhetorical devices as puns and anagrams into verses rife with biblical allusions rendered Mather's early poetry, at times, unnecessarily opaque. But from a historical standpoint, the elegies offered an intriguing, if biased, view of the esteem afforded one by his contemporaries at the time of death. They also offer evidence of Mather's extensive knowledge of classical and Renaissance literature, rooted in his early education. Even before entering Harvard at the age of eleven, Mather had supplemented his basic education by availing himself of the books in his father's substantial library. Between his public school education and his independent studies, Mather read extensively from Homer, Ovid, Virgil, Cicero, Horace, Erasmus, Descartes, and Milton and became fluent in Latin and competent in Hebrew and Greek. Mather's frequent references to classical figures in his elegies on Oakes and Cheever reveal not only his mastery of the authors and their works, but also demonstrates the respect he felt for the learned men who so profoundly influenced his youth. In any event, the poetry Mather would produce later in life was decidedly more appealing.

In contrast to his elegies on Oakes and Collins, the epitaph on Shubael Dummer and the elegies on Sarah Leveret and Mary Brown show a more mature poet fully in control of the elegiac form. In all three instances, Mather uses a much more sympathetic posture than in the earlier verses. The twenty-four line epitaph on Shubael Dummer, pastor of the church at York, Maine, adheres more closely to the true epitaphic tradition. While his heavy use of biblical allusion and his depiction of Dummer as a *"Bird of Paradise, Shot,* and *Flown* thither in a trice . . ."[32] obscures the facts of his death (Dummer was slain by Indians), Mather nevertheless celebrates Dummer's piety and preserves his dignity in a way that the earlier verse does not.

Of the fifty-six extant poems written by Mather in English, only three, written between 1702 and 1704, celebrate the virtues of women. Each is a posthumous tribute. These three poems are important not because of artistic merit, but because they provide some fascinating insight into the social status afforded individual Puritan women. In his long elegy on Sarah Leveret, written to commemorate the deceased wife of the late Massachusetts Governor John Leveret, Mather is uncharacteristically commendatory.[33] By alluding to "the *Heroines* that in past Times have been," Mather placed Sarah in a league with the biblical figure Miriam (sister of Moses), Deborah (judge and prophetess in the Old Testament renowned for her ability to settle disputes among the Israelites), Hannah (mother of the prophet Samuel), Dorcas (so honored for her good work and deeds that she was restored to life after death), and Mary.

Much of Mather's rhetoric was directed at young New England women, urging them to espouse the word of God, to avoid unwise companionship, to read religious rather than vile books, and to attend church rather than tempting social events. The exhortational tone he employed as a rhetorical device reinforced the didactic nature of the verse, and is evident when he admonishes his young audience not to engage in gambling:

> *Foul Cards* let your *Fair Hands* throw by with Scorn
> But *Write* and *Work* as for high purpose born.

That women should be granted the privilege of writing was also somewhat of an anomaly in colonial New England, although it is obvious that Mather did not view it as a female vocation. On the contrary, he still defined appropriate roles for women on everything from dress to eligibility for marriage:

> And in a *Body* clad with comely Dress,
> *Soul* drest with rich *Robes of Righteousness.*
> Thus did our admirable SARAH: Thus
> Of *Virgin-Grace* a mould she left for us.
> Her *Matchless Merits* now prepared her
> To be a *Match* for a great GOVERNOUR.

Not only was Sarah "lovely, discreet, and kind," but she was also revered by the community for her wisdom, her maternity, and her bravery in widowhood. Indeed, because she was such a public figure, Sarah Leveret was, for Mather, the ideal woman to be elegized.

"An Elegy Upon the Death of Mrs. Mary Brown" is perhaps one of Mather's best.[34] Written to commemorate a devout parishioner who died while giving birth, the poem is sincere and moving. Early in the verse, Mather establishes her (as he does Sarah Leveret) as a virtuous woman and enumerates her qualities of piety, learning, ambition, and industry. But Mather applauds even more enthusiastically her virtue as an "unpainted woman":

> *Pale* with the Fear of doing ill, and *Red*
> With Modesty, was all the *Paint* She had.

And then, about a hundred lines later:

> Sincere, She *Paint* abhorr'd; a *Jezabel*
> May *Paint*, but *Meat* unto the *Doggs* she fell.

Such a direct equation of physical purity with spiritual purity is somewhat unusual in Mather's verse: the implication is nearly always present but is usually obscured by a more subtle allusion. The reference is even more fascinating when one considers that he acknowledges but does not condemn Mary's penchant for fine accouterments:

> Sir, Tho' you *Cloath'd* her as you *Lov'd* her, well,
> She would of *You*, more than her *Cloathing* tell.

Still, later in the verse, there is another allusion to her generosity in donating food and clothes to charity:

> *Banquets* not in the *Hall*, but at the Door
> She still preferr'd, there for to feed the *Poor.*
> Her *old Cloaths*, on the *Poor*, a Neater Shew
> She judg'd, they made than of *her Self* her *New.*

Rather than diminishing the quality of the poetry, the allusion to clothing and cosmetics offers the contemporary reader a rare glimpse at the Puritan standards of appearance and dress.

A far more intriguing aspect of the poem, however, is that Mather comes as close as he ever does to creating sensual verse:

> Blame not the *Rabbi's* now for what they Write,
> How Heav'n did *Adam* and *Eve*, at first Unite.

> *Two Bodies* then if Heav'n in *One* did frame,
> *Two Souls* here met in *One* united Flame.

The allusion to the union of bodies and souls is vaguely reminiscent of Bradstreet's poem "To My Dear and Loving Husband," where she writes, "If ever two were one, then surely we."[35] While the allusion in Bradstreet's poem seems natural and even anticipatory, the similar passage in Mather's verse is uncharacteristic but nonetheless refreshing. The Brown elegy ends, however, in typical Mather fashion, with the author humbly acknowledging the shortcomings in his "Imperfect Verse."

In contrast with his long elegiac verse in which he rather rigidly adheres to a prescribed "form," Mather wrote perhaps one of his loveliest and most memorable verses on the death of his long-time wife, Abigail, who died after a long illness. In the 14-line poem, distributed initially as a broadside at her funeral, Mather pays tender tribute to his wife of sixteen years. He refers to her as "my DOVE," and cites the anguish caused by her death, not only for himself, but for her many friends. Abigail had played an integral and essential part in Mather's life, and the poem captures not only his remorse, but also his unconditional acceptance of her death:

> Go then, my DOVE, but now no longer *mine;*
> Leave *Earth,* and now in *heavenly Glory* shine.
> *Bright* for thy Wisdome, Goodness, Beauty here;
> Now *brighter* in a more *angelic* Sphære
> JESUS, with whom thy Soul did long to be,
> Into his *Ark,* and Arms, has taken thee. . . .[36]

Mather's consolation stems in part from his belief that heaven will hold for his wife an even brighter existence than did life on earth. But the greater consolation arises at the end of the poem when Mather echoes Abigail's last spoken words, "HEAV'N, HEAV'N WILL MAKE AMENDS FOR ALL." The reaffirmation of his faith allows Mather to alleviate his grief. And unlike Anne Bradstreet, Mather doesn't question the justice of the action before reconciling himself to the loss. Moreover, he demonstrates a sensitivity rarely seen in his works. Even the poem "My Satisfaction" written on the death of his infant son, Samuel, lacks the tenderness and emotion that characterize the epitaph to his wife. Instead, Mather simply urges his son to be at peace in God's custody.

While the death of a loved one most often falls into what some critics term "private" poetry, the line between public and private modes for Mather is blurred.[37] The fact that a substantial amount of his diary and *Paterna* verse found its way into publication during his lifetime suggests that the poetry was not so much an exercise in self-expression for Mather as it was a means of promoting religious truth. "Go then, my Dove," while certainly the most personal of all his lyrics, was not only distributed to mourners at Abigail's funeral but later appeared as one of several verses in Mather's *Meat Out of the Eater.* That Mather was a public figure dedicated to the promotion of religious truths might explain why much of his otherwise "private" poetry was fit for public consumption.

Mather's later poetry is, in general, better than his earlier verse. He achieves more control over his subject, and his poetry is devoid of the strained conceits that characterize much of his earlier work. In a diary entry made three years before his death at the age of sixty-five, the image of a sad and lonely man in broken health emerges:

> When I sitt alone in my Languishments, unable to write, or to read, I often compose little Hyms [*sic*], agreeable unto my present Circumstances, and sing them unto the Lord. . . . Having found my Mind for some time without such precious and impressive Thoughts of GOD my SAVIOUR, as are the Life of my Spirit, I thus mourn'd and sang unto the Lord.[38]

The verse that follows, "O Glorious CHRIST of GOD; I live" (the last diary verse Mather ever wrote) is as enlightening as it is inspirational. Appealing to God for restoration of not only his physical health but his broken spirits, Mather produces an exceptional hymn that rivals "Go then, my Dove" as a legitimate and emotive verse. Both verses, which are among Mather's finest, served an important personal function as he faced immensely difficult losses.

As happens with "O Glorious CHRIST . . . ," the six poems from *Agricola. Or, the Religious Husbandman* (1727) depart from Mather's earlier work.[39] The heavy symbolic use of at least two of the natural elements (earth and water) does not detract from what are simple and delightful little verses. In "Singing at the Plow," Mather uses the thick and stiffened soil as a metaphor for his hardened heart:

> My *Heart*, how very *Hard* its grown!
> Thicken'd and stiffen'd Clay:
> Daily trod by the *Wicked One*;
> Of *Sin* the *Beaten Way.*

An *Heart*, wherein compacted *Weeds*
Of *Diverse Lusts* abound;
No Entrance for the Heavenly Seeds,
Falling on such a Ground!

Freeing his heart of "compacted *Weeds*," however, would result in a purification of the soul; thus, the process of weeding will once again allow spiritual growth. The plow in this verse becomes a symbol for God's message, and in a play on words Mather pleads with Him to "let thy SPIRIT drive it home."

Another verse in the *Agricola* series, "The Rain gasped for," reinforces the Puritan notion that everything on earth, including drought, is a result of God's divine providence. But this verse has a double meaning. Not only is Mather appealing to God for actual precipitation in the form of rain, but more importantly, the rain becomes a metaphor for religious inspiration. There is an implicit analogy between the evaporation of the land's much needed moisture and the thirst for religious truth on earth. The symbolism grows stronger in each successive line, and by stanza six, the need for spiritual rebirth is explicit:

Yea, come upon a World forlorn,
And with a Quickening *Dew*,
Make thou Mankind, of *Water* born,
Tho' *Dead*, their *Life* Renew.

Mather ends the verse by reaffirming that until the "drought" is lifted, the ministers will do the best they can to ensure dissemination of religious truth.

Another poem from *Agricola*, "The Sons of GOD, Singing among The Trees of GOD," uses a tree as a metaphor for the soul. Based on passages from Genesis 2:9 and Revelation 2:7, the poem symbolically compares a barren tree to a barren soul, which only through the grace of God will escape being "thrown down to Hell." The speaker appeals to his "Saviour" to transform him into a "Tree of Righteousness: fill'd with . . . Fruits," so that even when the tree eventually falls and dies, it will transcend earth and be "*transplanted* to thy *Paradise*" where it will continue to flourish.

In contrast with his other late-life poetry, or with any verse Mather ever produced, is the enigmatic 26-line piece entitled "The Pidgeon Py. A Poem in Imitation of the Monumental Gratitude." Written during the last year of Mather's life, the poem is a parody of John Hubbard's 1727 verse describing the trials of several Yale students caught in a raging storm on Long Island Sound. Appearing in a copy of the publication, the sometimes indecipherable poem, inscribed in Mather's hand on the title page and inside cover, describes the impatient anticipation and subsequent gorging of the pie by an apparently famished crew. Mather parodies not only Hubbard's subject, but his style as well, dipping and raising his words near the end of the poem in imitation of the waves that punctuate Hubbard's verse. Why Mather should make such a radical departure from his usual form and whether the poem is a condemnation of Hubbard's style, or a product of Mather's serious illness, remains a mystery.

The majority of Mather's other poems, in contrast to those discussed above, were written for the purpose of versifying doctrine for the sake of instruction. While the *Agricola* poems relied heavily on metaphors, for instance, Mather's sole intention in writing verse for children was to make doctrine accessible and understandable. By versifying such material as "The Lord's Prayer" and "The Ten Commandments," Mather simplified the sometimes awesome task of absorbing religious doctrine that was expected of children. Transforming theology into intelligible verse enhanced its didactic function; for instance, Mather made the value of adhering to religious convictions perfectly clear in a short poem using a child's voice to describe another child's death:

> I in the *Burying Place* may see
> *Graves* not so long as I.
> From *Deaths Arrest* no Age is free;
> *Young Children* too may Dy.
> *My God,* may such an awful sight
> Awakening be to me!
> Oh! that by *Early Grace* I might
> For *Death* prepared be.[40]

Another device Mather used in children's poems was to transcribe biblical passages into comprehensible verse. Psalm 119:9, for example, which reads: "Wherewithal shall a young man cleanse his way? by taking heed *THERETO* according to thy word," becomes in Mather's hand:

> May I, while I am *Young,* give Heed
> Unto thy *Holy* Word;
> Call'd, there to *Cleanse* my wayes with Speed,
> By the most *Holy Lord.*[41]

Unfortunately, no copy of Mather's *Good Lessons for Children,* first published in 1706 as a text and used extensively by Puritan youth, is known to have survived. In a diary entry from March 1705–6, Mather recounts the circumstances leading to its publication. Originally intended as an aid for his young son, Mather soon realized that other children could benefit as well:

> My Proposal was, to have the Child improve in *Goodness* at the same time, that he improv'd in *Reading.* Upon further Thoughts, I apprehended, that a Collection of some of them would be serviceable to the Good Education of other Children. So I lett the Printer take them, and print them, in some hope of some Help is thereby contributed unto that great Intention of a *good Education.*[42]

Mather modestly alludes to its immediate success with the brief parenthetical notation, "It quickly has a second Edition." The book was, in fact, in print as late as 1722 or 23.[43] In his preface to "The Body of Divinity Versifyed," Mather again notes the utilitarian purpose of poetry for youth and its pious implications: "The CHRISTIAN RELIGION, will not be the less *Relishable* to, or the less *Retainable* by, the Faculties of Young People for being set before them under the Advantage of *Poetry.*" Once again, poetry has served a useful end.

One might be tempted to attribute the roughness of Mather's poetic style to time that was better spent on other endeavors, particularly on those numerous sermons and historical works for which he is renowned. Mather nonetheless deserves recognition as a minor poet. While his lyrics clearly lack the warmth and compassion of Anne Bradstreet's better poetry, the sensuous and emotional impulse of Edward Taylor's verse, and the dramatic religious fervor characteristic of Michael Wigglesworth's poetry, they measure well against those of other minor poets as representative of at least one type of colonial verse. Early in Mather's career, a person corresponding with his father remarked of Cotton's poetic attempts, "in my thoughts he will never win the laurel of his poesy."[44] Nearly three hundred years later, Thomas J. Holmes expressed similar sentiments when he noted: "As a singer of poetry Cotton Mather's verse is hoarse. His songs lack lilt and sweetness."[45] Despite what they may lack in artistic merit, Cotton Mather's verses nevertheless make a unique and significant contribution to our understanding of the Puritan imagination.

Notes

1. *Diary of Cotton Mather,* ed. Worthington Chauncey Ford (New York, n.d.), 2:242.

2. See Robert Daly's "In Critic's Hands: A Bibliographical Essay" in *God's Altar: The World and the Flesh in Puritan Poetry* (Berkeley and Los Angeles: University of California Press, 1978). In a 23-page appendix, Daly chronologically summarizes the views of more than a dozen critics of Puritan poetry.

3. Cotton Mather, "Of Poetry and Style," from *Manuductio ad Ministerium* in *The Puritans,* ed. Perry Miller and Thomas H. Johnson (New York: Harper and Row, 1963), 2:686–87.

4. Daly, "In Critic's Hands," p. 210.

5. Kenneth Silverman, *Colonial American Poetry* (New York: Hafner, 1968), p. 33.

6. *Manuductio,* p. 688.

7. Ibid., p. 687.

8. Ibid., p. 688.

9. Ibid.

10. Ibid., pp. 684–85.

11. Ibid., p. 686.

12. Ibid.

13. Harrison T. Meserole, *Seventeenth-Century American Poetry* (New York: New York University Press, 1968), p. xxiv.

14. Richard Mather, preface to *The Bay Psalm Book,* in *The Puritans,* ed. Perry Miller and Thomas H. Johnson (New York: Harper and Row, 1963), 2:672.

15. Cotton Mather, *Magnalia Christi Americana* (1702), ed. Thomas Robbins (Hartford, 1852), 2:406.

16. Meserole, *Seventeenth-Century American Poetry* p. xxi.

17. Silverman, *Colonial American Poetry,* p. 129.

18. Ibid., p. 128.

19. Cotton Mather, "A Poem Dedicated to the Memory of the Reverend and Excellent Mr. Urian Oakes" (Boston, 1682).

20. Cotton Mather, "An Elegy On the Much-to-be-deplored Death of that Never-to-be-forgotten Person, the Reverend Mr. Nathanael Collins" (Boston, 1685).

21. "A Poem . . . to . . . Oakes."

22. Silverman, *Colonial American Poetry,* p. 124.

23. "A Poem . . . to . . . Oakes."

24. "An Elegy On . . . Collins."

25. Ibid.

26. *Magnalia,* 2:32.

27. "A Poem . . . to . . . Oakes."

28. "An Elegy On . . . Collins."

29. A collection of essays tracing the development and application of typological exegesis appears in Sacvan Bercovitch's *Typology and Early American Literature* (N.p.: University of Massachusetts Press, 1972).

30. "A Poem . . . to . . . Oakes."

31. "An Elegy On . . . Collins."

32. Cotton Mather, "Epitaph" (on Shubael Dummer) in *Fair Weather* (Boston, 1691), pp. 92–3.

33. Cotton Mather, "A Lacrymatory: Design'd for the Tears let fall at the Funeral of Mrs. Sarah Leveret" in *Monica Americana* (Boston, 1705), pp. 29–32.

34. Cotton Mather, "An Elegy Upon the Death of Mrs. Mary Brown" in *Eureka. The Vertuous Woman Found* (Boston, 1704), pp. 1–8.

35. Anne Bradstreet, "To My Dear and loving Husband" in *The Works of Anne*

26

Bradstreet, ed. Jeannine Hensley (Cambridge: Harvard University Press, Belknap Press, 1967), p. 225.

36. C. Mather, *Diary,* 1:450.

37. For a fine discussion of the dichotomy between the public and private spheres in Puritan poetry, see Agnieszka Salska's "Puritan Poetry: Its Public and Private Strain" in *Early American Literature* 19 (1984): 107–20.

38. C. Mather, *Diary,* 2:786.

39. Cotton Mather, *Agricola. Or, The Religious Husbandman* (Boston, 1727).

40. Cotton Mather, "Instructions for Children" in *The A, B, C. of Religion* (Boston, 1713), pp. 37–42.

41. Cotton Mather, "Early Religion" in "A Token for the Children of New England," appended to James Janeway's *A Token for Children* (Boston, 1700), pp. 29–30.

42. C. Mather, *Diary,* 1:555–56.

43. Harold S. Jantz, *The First Century of New England Verse* (New York: Russell and Russell, 1943), p. 231.

44. Kenneth Silverman, *The Life and Times of Cotton Mather* (New York: Harper and Row, 1984), p. 38.

45. Thomas J. Holmes, *Cotton Mather: A Bibliography of His Works,* 3 vols. (Cambridge: Massachusetts Historical Society, 1940), 1:32.

A Note on the Text

The purpose of this edition is to bring together for the first time into one volume all complete extant poems of Cotton Mather written in English. The only exceptions I have made are to exclude couplets and one-line verse (which are primarily translations from Latin or adaptations from classical sources), complete volumes of verse translated from Latin, such as *Psalterium Americanum*, short verse scattered throughout the *Magnalia Christi Americana*, for which there is no compelling or verifiable evidence of Mather's authorship, and verse in the "Biblia Americana," which Mather attributes to other authors. In all, fifty-six verses have been collected. Representative of verse I have chosen to exclude is the following couplet, translated from Latin in Mather's *Nehemiah. A Brief Essay on Divine Consolations* (Boston, 1710):

> Soul, whom the Worlds Fatigues do make to groan,
> See, all they Comfort in they GOD alone.

Such verse is not a significant enough poetic expression to merit inclusion into what is otherwise a collection of Mather's more noteworthy endeavors.

Texts for this edition have been drawn primarily from three sources: the original printings of Mather's verse which are collected and reproduced in the Early American Imprints Microcards Series, Mather's two-volume *Diary*, and his autobiography, *Paterna*. In some instances, however, it was necessary to consult an original published edition for verification of text that was otherwise unclear. The bibliography listing Cotton Mather's poetry in Harold S. Jantz's *The First Century of New England Verse* served as my primary source for locating the poetry texts; in only a few instances did I discover material that was not listed by Jantz. A bibliography supplementing Jantz's is appended to my text.

In all cases, I used the earliest printed edition as my primary text; subsequent editions are collated and variations noted by line

29

number in a separate section entitled "Textual Notes." Any editorial emendations, which have been kept to an absolute minimum, are also documented in the "Textual Notes." On those rare occasions where it was impossible to reconstruct text because of damaged or mutilated copy, a note has been provided to that effect.

Mather's capitalization, spelling, punctuation, indentations, brackets, and italics have been preserved. The only liberties I have taken with the text have been to replace the old-style long *s* with a modern *s* and to eliminate ornamental and bold letter usage. In addition, the catch word appearing at the bottom of each page signaling the first word of the following page has not been retained, and bracketed titles have been supplied to indicate that Mather left a verse untitled. The only other change I have made is to include line numbers beginning on line 5 and on every fifth line thereafter to assist the reader in locating editorial emendations and textual variations. My objective has been to reproduce the original text rather than to "improve" it through modernization.

In addition to "Textual Notes," Mather's own notes have been retained in a separate "Notes" section; they are indicated by a bracketed "Mather's note." Where further elucidation is needed to clarify Mather's note, I have followed the bracket with an explanation. Allusions to obscure biblical figures, places, classical figures, events, words, and other information have also been noted when necessary to make the text comprehensible to the reader.

This edition is organized into six sections, and the poems are presented chronologically within each section. Often, the verse could be classified two or even more ways; it is at times difficult to distinguish, for example, between hymns and biblical translations not intended for singing. To the extent possible, however, I have attempted to group the poems in a way that most prominently reveals their common features.

An appendix containing verse that appeared in Mather's diaries and his autobiography, *Paterna,* is also included. In those cases where *Diary* and *Paterna* verses were published separately during Mather's lifetime, a cross reference to the published version has been provided and variations in the texts noted. A section containing inscriptions in Mather's hand is also appended.

Some of Mather's verse has failed to survive. In addition to *Good Lessons for Children,* mentioned in the Introduction, copies of at least three other verses have been lost. One, "A Poem of Consolations under Blindness," was written for an "aged and pious Gentlewoman, visited with total Blindness," according to Mather in a

30

diary entry dated 20 November 1701. Another more substantial work that is missing is a body of hymns entitled *Songs of the Redeemed*, which was referenced in Samuel Mather's list of his father's publications. There was also a copy of the text in the library of William Adams at Yale College in 1726, according to information on file at the Massachusetts Historical Society (4 Coll. M. H. S., vol. I, p. 44). Finally, the Massachusetts Historical Society also has on file a letter from Thomas Hollis to Samuel Mather dated 27 July 1727 suggesting that Mather may have written a poem on eyeglasses that has been lost. I have attempted, however, to compile a full and complete edition of Mather's extant verse, with the few exceptions noted earlier.

Cotton Mather's
Verse in English

Part One: Religious Meditations

The Body of Divinity Versifyed.

A God there is, a God of boundless Might,
In Wisdom, Justice, Goodness, Infinite.
God is but One and yet in Persons Three.
The *Father, Son,* and *Spirit,* One God we see.
Our God, by His Great Name JEHOVAH known,   5
HE the *World* Made, and Keeps, and Rules Alone.
To Glorify the Glorious *God,* is That
For which He did all men, and me Create.
God a Just *Rule* doth in our *Bible* give,
A Rule, both what to *Think,* and how to *Live.*   10
Holy & Happy our First Parents came
From Gods Hand, with Gods Image in our Frame.
Tasting *Forbidden Fruit* our Parents fell;
This *Taste* has plung'd Mankind all down to *Hell.*
Our Blest Lord JESUS CHRIST, in our Distress,   15
Comes to *fetch* us from *Hell to Blessedness.*
Into his Person, the Bright *Son of God,*
A Virgins Son took; There He makes *Abode.*
Life as a Priest CHRIST will His People bring,
Light as a Prophet, & *Law* as a King.   20
For us our *Surety* Liv'd, for us he Dy'd,
And Rising did to Heaven in *Triumph* Ride.
By *Faith* to *Christ* we for *Salvation* go;
Faith too, as well as *That* must He bestow.
For *Sin* will the Renew'd Believer *Mourn,*   25
And from all *Sin,* he'l by Repentance *Turn.*
Sinners receiving of *Gods Pardon,* they
Gods Precept will, made *Saints,* with *Love* Obey.
All *Homage* we must yield unto the *Lord;*
In all directed, by His *Heavenly Word.*   30
His Works and Names, we may not use in Vain;
Nor by our *Works* thereon His Days Profane.
With Honours due we must our Neighbours treat;
And sweetly wish them Lives both *Long & Sweet.*
With Chastity we must our selves Behave;   35

And do no Wrong in what we Get or Save.
Truth we must utter, & abhor to Lye;
And be Content, tho' in Adversity.
Them who to be in CHRIST, thro' *Grace,* Consent,
God brings into His *Gracious Covenant.*   40
The *Baptism* of the *Lord,* assures that we
Both *Wash'd* from *Sin,* & *Rais'd* from *Death,* shall be.
To *See* the Lord, we at His *Table* Sitt,
And Show, that we shall in His *Kingdom* Eat.
Gods Children His good *Promises* Enjoy: 45
And *Good* comes of what *Ill* may them annoy.
His Angels He to them does *Guardians* make,
And these their *Souls,* at their Departure take.
To Judge the World, CHRIST will descend at Last;
A Righteous *Doom* shall by that *Judge* be past.   50
The Wicked shall bear bitter *Pain* and *Shame,*
With *Wicked Spirits* in Eternal Flame.
The Godly shall, with their Great GOD, on High,
Reap *Joyes,* High *Joyes,* to all Eternity.

Conversion Exemplified.

AND now, to Life Rais'd by the Heav'nly Call,
Henceforth *Vain Idols,* I Renounce you all.
    Vile *Flesh,* Thy raging *Lust,* and sordid *Ease,*
My winged Soul now shall not serve and please.
    False *World,* Thy *Laws* shall be no longer mine,   5
Nor to thy *Wayes* my New-born *Soul* incline.
    Satan, Thou wilt, I know, my *Tempter* be;
But thy *Temptation* shall not Govern me.
    Foolish I've been; *O Lord,* I blush, I grieve;
And gladly would my *Woful Folly* leave.   10
Fain would I *Turn* to God; but can't alone:
Help, *Sovereign Grace,* or it will ne'er be done!
To the Great GOD of Heaven I repair,
And Help'd by Heaven, thus to Him declare.
    Great GOD, Since to be *Mine* Thou willing art,   15
Oh! Be Thou mine! Replies my Conquered Heart.
To Glorify Thee, *Glorious Lord,* I take,
For *That* alone, which can me *Happy* make.

O FATHER, of all Things *Creator* Great,
Wilt thou all Happiness for me *Create?*   20
Eternal SON of God, Wilt thou me *Save,*
That I the *Hopes* may of a *Gods Children* have?
Eternal SPIRIT of God, Poor me wilt thou
With *Spiritual Blessings* of all sorts Endow?
Lord, Ravish'd at thy wondrous *Grace,* I do   25
These *Gracious Offers* now Conform unto.
    O *All-sufficient* ONE, Wilt thou supply
My Wants from Stores of rich *Immensity?*
Shall Boundless *Wisdome* for my *Good* Contrive?
And Boundless *Power* ye Fruits of *Goodness* Give?   30
Shall Spotless *Holiness* on me Imprint,
An *Holy Temper,* with thine *Image* in't?
Lord, Thy *Perfections* all I do adore,
And to a *Perfect Love* my mind would soar.

A *State of BLISS*, according to thy Word   35
Thou wilt unto thy Chosen Ones afford.
A State of Blissful *Rest* and *Joy,* wherein
Rais'd from the *Dead*, they shall be freed from *Sin.*
There Bath'd in Rivers of Eternal *Joy,*
No *Sorrows* more shall them at all annoy.   40
GOD shall be *All in All;* Brought nigh to God,
In *Him* they shall forever make Abode.
They shall *See God;* The *Beatific Sight*
And *their own God* shall take in them Delight.
    My Soul, Make now thy Choice. O say; Is This   45
What thou dost Choose for thy Chief Blessedness?
Things of this *Present Time!* now Refuse;
My Blessed GOD, Thee, *Thee,* and *This,* I Chuse.
May the sweet JESUS me to *Glory* bring,
And be my Glorious *Prophet, Priest,* and *King.*   50
    Does the Almighty SON of God, to those
That *Will*, an *Union* with Himself propose?
My Lord, I will! The *Will* thou didst bestow:
To Thee, Oh, Let me be *United* so.

The full *Obedience* which my *Surety* paid   55
To God, may *That* my *Righteousness* be made.
A *Wretched* Sinner would appear in *That,*
Righteous before the dreadful *Judgment-Seat.*

Show me *thy Way*, O *Lord*, Lest that I shou'd
Fall by those *Mockers* that will me delude.   60
To thy Pure *Scriptures-Way* I will adhere,
And find the *Rule* of my whole Conduct there.
  All the *Rebellion* of my Heart Subdue;
And for *thy* work, O *Lord*, my *Strength* Renew.
From thy vast *Fulness* let my *Faith* derive   65
Strength to do all things, and to Thee to Live.

May thy *Good* SPIRIT me Possess, and Fill
With *Light* and *Zeal*, to Learn and Do thy Will.
With His Kind *Flames* may He upon me Sieze [*sic*],
And keep me alwayes on my *Bended Knees*.   70
May all I am and have, be us'd for Him
Whose is my *All*, for *He* did me Redeem.
To Thee, *Good SPIRIT*, I lift up my Cries,
That thou wilt fall upon the *Sacrifice*.
  May thy Bright ANGELS, be my *Guardians* then;   75
For Thee, they'l *Guard* and *Guide* the Sons of Men.
By Thee assisted, LORD, Thus I Consent
Unto thy Everlasting COVENANT.

My Satisfaction.[1]

From *Heb. XII.* 5,6,11.

The *Exhortation* of the Lord,
With *Consolation* speaks to us;
As unto His *Children*, His Good Word,
We must *Remember* Speaking Thus,

My Child, When God shall Chasten Thee,   5
His Chastning do thou not contemn:
When thou His just Rebukes dost see,
Faint not Rebuked under them.

The Lord with Fit *Afflictions* will
Correct the *Children* of His *Love;*   10
He doth Himself their *Father* still,
By His most wise *Corrections* prove.

Afflictions for the present here
The vexed *Flesh* will *Grievous* call;
But *Afterward* there will appear,   15
Not *Grief,* but *Peace,* the End of all.

My Resignation.
[From *Heb.* 11.17. with *Gen.* 22.12.]

The Dearest Lord of *Heaven* gave
Himself an *Offering* once for me:
The Dearest Thing on *Earth* I have,
Now, Lord, I'll offer unto Thee.

I *see* my best Enjoyments here,   5
Are *Loans,* and *Flow'rs,* and *Vanities;*
E're well *Enjoy'd* they disappear:
Vain *Smoke,* they prick and leave our *Eyes.*

But I *Believe,* O Glorious Lord,
That when I seem to *Lose* these *Toyes,*   10
What's *Lost* will fully be Restor'd
In Glory, with Eternal *Joyes.*

I do *Believe,* That I and mine,
Shall come to *Everlasting Rest;*
Because, *Blest Jesus,* we are Thine,   15
And with thy *Promises* are *Blest.*

I do *Believe,* That ev'ry *Bird*
Of mine, which to the Ground shall fall,
Does fall at thy kind *Will* and *Word;*
Nor *I,* nor *It,* is hurt at all.   20

Now my *Believing Soul* does Hear
This among the Glad *Angels* told;
I know, thou dost thy Maker Fear,
From whom thou nothing dost withold!

My Resolution.

Job I. 21. *Naked came I out of my Mothers womb, and Naked shall I return thither: The Lord gave, and the Lord hath taken away; Blessed be the Name of the Lord.*

I Strip't of *Earthly* Comforts am:
   Strip't let me duely Mourn:
Naked from *Earth* at first I came;
   And *Naked* I return.

What, but *Gifts* from Above were they?   5
   GOD *gave* them unto me.
And now they *Take* their Flight away,
   Taken by GOD they be.

The Name of my great GOD, I will
   For ever then Adore: 10
HEE'S *Wise*, and *Just*, and *Sov'raign* still,
   And *Good* for ever more.

Songs in Such a Night.

Psal: 42.5,11.
Oppress'd with Loads of *Grief* Art thou
My Soul, O why dejected so?
Why do thy *Grevious passions* now
Into a Restless Tumult grow!

In *God* thy *Hope* Rejoycing place;   5
My God He is by Covenant;
I'll *praise* Him still: *Joy* to *my Face*
The *Help* of *His* will surely grant.

I Sam. 1.15,18.
My *Spirit* is, how *Sorrowful!*
But Lord, I do *pour out* before   10
Thy Grace the *Sorrows* of my Soul;
And now I will be *Sad no more.*

I Pet. 1.8.

The CHRIST I *see* not, yet I *know,*
I *Trust* and *Love;* Thro' CHRIST there is given
A *Joy unutterable* to   15
My *Faith,* a *Joy* that's *full of Heaven.*

My Text Paraphrased, and Faith Exhibited.

GODS Son *Incarnate,* now *Akin*
    To miserable me,
From all the *Miseries* of *Sin*
    Sets me at Libertie.

By His full *Price* to Justice paid,   5
    my Bonds of *Death* are Eas'd:
By His Great Pow'r thereon display'd,
    Deaths Prisoner is Releas'd.

That the Almighty JESUS is
    My own Redeemer now,   10
By my Consenting to be *His,*
    On Terms of *Grace,* I know.

I *Know* that my Redeemer *Lives;*
    His *Grave* detain'd Him not;
Enthron'd, from His High *Throne* He gives,   15
    What in His *Grave* He bought.

And now, I *know* that all He said,
    must be for ever True;
His being *Risen from the Dead*
    His glorious *Truth* doth shew.   20

I *Know,* when I or Mine shall *Dy,*
    We shall to *Heaven* go;
Since our *Fore-runner Lives* on High
    concern'd for us below.

[Go then, my Dove]¹

Go then, my Dove, but now no longer *Mine!*
Leave *Earth,* & now in *Heavenly Glory* Shine.
Bright for thy Wisdom, Goodness, Beauty here;
Now *Brighter* in a more *Angelick Sphære.*
JESUS, with whom thy Soul did long to be,   5
Into His *Ark,* and Arms, has taken thee.
Dear *Friends* with whom thou didst so dearly Live,
Feel *Thy one Death* to *Them* a *Thousand* give.
Thy *Prayers* are done; thy *Alms* are spent; thy *Pains*
Are *Ended* now in *Endless* Joyes & Gains.   10
The *Torch* that gave my *House* its pleasant *Light,*
Extinguish'd leaves it in how *dark* a *Night!*
  I faint, till thy last words to mind I call;
Rich Words! Heav'n, Heav'n will make amends for all.

The Language of a SOUL taken in,
The Nets of Salvation.

Grace Irresistible subdues me, Lord;
And I no longer can *Resist* thy Word.

  My SOUL too long lies in its Grave forgot;
Whose price bright *Pearls,* yea, whole *Worlds*
      Equal not:
A SOUL whereto GOD such Respect ha's had;   5
And which *Repenting,* would make *Angels* glad.

  I *Loathe & Leave* now all the Paths of SIN,
And *Mourn* that I have stray'd so long therein.
The Paths of True *Religion* I prefer,
As what most Just & Good & Lovely are.   10

O Great JEHOVAH, Thou *my God* shalt be;
And I my ALL surrender unto thee.
My *Life* is in thy *FAVOUR;* Let me live
In *That,* & to thy Name all *Glory* give.

  Be though my Father, O Thou *Three in One,*   15
My Saviour be, my Leader, Thou alone.

Oh! May I know, & Love, & serve my God,
And *fill'd* with Him, in Him have my Abode.
    I won't believe what the *Destroyer* sayes,
Nor will I walk in his *Destructive* wayes.   20

    Thee, O my SAVIOUR, with a *Lively* Faith,
I ask to *Save* me from Eternal *Death.*
Me now Resign'd to thy most Glorious Hands;
Free by thy *Merits, Rule* by thy *Commands.*
    O *Wisdom,* open thou my Sinful Eyes;   25
And with a *Light* from Heaven make me wise.
O *Righteous* One, let thy *Obedience* paid
To God for me, my *Righteousness* be made.
    O *Holy* One, my Heart inflame with *Zeal,*
In Flights of *Holiness* to do thy Will.   30
O *Strong Redeemer,* Help a wretched *Slave,*
And from *Deaths Chains* let me *Redemption* have.

Lord, Me to thy *Caelestial City* bring,
Where thy dear *Saints* behold no grievous thing
There let me *See,* & with the *Sight,* possess   35
My JESUS, in Compleat and Endless Bliss.
In Hope of that Rich Bliss, I will despise
This *Vain World,* and its *Lying Vanities.*
                              FINIS

The Consent.
In imitation of the Virgin's Answer to the Angel.

[Luk. i.38.]

Great GOD: Thy *Chosen* People shall
Each one to Thee be *Called* home:
And to a *Choice* of thee they All
On thy Heart-conq'ring *Call* shall come.

God, *Father, Son,* and *Spirit,* make   5
Tenders that overcome us quite:

I'll be your GOD; He sayes: *I'll take*
In you, as in dear Sons delight.

The *Lord-Redeemer* does propose
To Pay for us a wondrous *Price;*   10
To guide our *Wayes;* to quell our *Foes;*
And Lodge us in Eternal *Bliss.*

Dissolv'd by such sweet Rayes of Grace,
Darted from Thee, most Gracious Lord;
Behold, Thy willing Servant Prayes,   15
Fulfil to me thy Glorious Word.

JESUS, Our Holy *Surety* did
Work out a *Righteousness* compleat;
Sinners, Tis yours, He sayes, *to Plead,*
Righteous before Gods Judgment-seat.   20

Our *Sin,* of Enemies the worst,
This, God will *Pardon* and *Subdue;*
Tis this, O God, for which I thirst!
Sins *Death,* Saints as their *Life* pursue.

When *Tempted,* our kind Friend on High,   25
Succours will send us down from thence;
To *Him,* we in *Temptations* fly;
And *Favours* Hee'l by them dispense.

Dissolv'd by such sweet Rayes of Grace,
Darted from Thee, most Gracious Lord;   30
Behold, Thy willing Servant Prayes,
Fulfill to me thy Glorious Word.

Our *Spirits* Born from *Heav'n* above,
God will for *Heav'nly Flights* prepare;
Then them to *Paradise* remove,   35
And *Blessed Visions* grant them there.

Our *Cleansed Bodies* from the *Grave,*
He to our *Spirits* will restore;
In them we shall *New Mansions* have,
Bright, Strong; And, *death shall be no more.*   40

So, in the CITY of our God,
Him we shall *Serve,* and *Love,* and *See:*
O *City* of our *Long* Abode;
How Long, till we arrive to thee!

Dissolv'd by such Sweet Rayes of Grace,   45
Darted from Thee, most Gracious Lord;
Behold, Thy willing Servant Prayes,
Fulfill to me thy Glorious Word.

Part Two: Elegies and Epitaphs

A POEM
Dedicated to the Memory
OF
The Reverend and Excellent
MR. *URIAN OAKES,*
the late Pastor to Christ's Flock,
and Præsident of Harvard-Colledge,
in Cambridge,
Who was gathered to his People on 25ᵈ 5ᵐᵒ 1681.
In the fifty'th Year of his Age.[1]

TO THE
R E A D E R.

Worthies *to* Praise *is a* Praise-worthy thing;
Christ *did it; and will do it! And to Sing*
The Elogyes *of Saints departed in*
The Rhythm *of* Elegyes, *has always been*
Esteemed Reason! David *bids me go*
My Christian Reader! and like him do so.

Cotton *Embalms great* Hooker; Norton *Him;*
And Norton's *Herse do's* Poet-Wilson *trim*
With Verses: Mitchel *writes a poem on*
The Death of Wilson; *And when* Mitchel's *gone,*
Shepard *with fun'ral Lamentations gives*
Honour to Him: and at his Death receives
The like from the [like-Maro][2]*Lofty Strain*
Of admirable Oakes![3] *I should be vain*
To thrust into that gallant Chorus: *Pride*
Ne'er made mee such an Icharus:[4] *I cry'd*
Of good Exemples [Ahimaaz[5] *his Thought*]
How if I should run after them? *And brought*
These as a Pattern, *and a* Plea *for what*

51

I do; that my cross Reader blame me not.
But why so late? *my* Nænia's *some will deem*
Both out of Time, *and* Tune! *To some I seem*
Grief's Resurrection *to essay; and bee*
Just like the Trojans *who came late to see*
And sorrow with Tiberius![6]—*Only this*
Shall be Reply'd! The fond Bookseller *is*
Now guilty of this Paper's Ravishment
When long supprest: Give him thy Discontent!
Since Oakes (*as* Homer) *has all Places* Claim;
Let Boston *too forget its* Anagram!

Memoirs
of the Life and Worth:
Lamentations
for the Death, and Loss
of
the every way admirable
Mr. URIAN OAKES.

Weep with me, Reader! Never *Poet* had
His Quill employ'd upon a *Theme* so sad
As what just Providence (Grief *grumble* not)
Do's with black *Warrant Press* mee to! O what?
This! *OAKES* is dead! One of the bittrest *Pills*   5
(*Compounded of three Monosyllables*)
That could have been dispensed! *Absalom*[7]
Sure felt not more *Distress, Death, Danger,* come
With the *three Darts of Joab!*————
Blest *Shade!* an *Universal Tax* of Sorrow   10
Thy Country ows thee! Ah! we need not borrow
The *Prasica's:* Say, *Oakes is dead!* and there!
There is enough to squeese a briny Tear
From the most flinty *Flint:* Once at the *Blow*
Of *Moses,* from a *Rock* a *Stream* did flow;   15
But look! th' *Almightye's Rod* now Smites us home
Oh! what *Man* won't a *Mourner* now become?
Dear Saint! I cannot but thy Herse bedew
With dropping of some *Fun'ral Tears!* I Rue

52

Thy Death! I must, *My Father*! *Father*! say,   20
Our Chariots and our Horsemen where are they?
I the *dumb son* of *Crasus*[8] 'fore mine Eyes
Have sett, and will *cry* when my *Father* dyes.
Oh! but a *Verse* to wait upon thy Grave,
A *Verse* our *Custome*, and thy *Friends* will have: 25
And must I *brue* my Tears? ah! shall I *fetter*
My Grief, by studying for to *mourn* in *Metre*?
Must too my *cloudy* Sorrows *rain* in *Tune*,
Distilling like the softly Showrs of *June*?
Alas! My *Ephialtes*[9] takes me! See't!   30
I strive to *run*, but then I want my *feet*.
What shall I do? Shall I go invocate
The *Muses* to mine aid? No, That I hate!
The Sweet *New England-Poet* rightly said,
It is a most Unchristian Use and Trade   35
Of Some that Christians would be thought.[10] If I
Call'd Help, the *Muses* mother *Memory*
Would be enough: He that *Remembers* well
The *Use* and *Loss* of *Oakes*, will grieve his fill.
Ih'd *rather* pray, that Hee, in whose just *Eyes*   40
The Death of his dear *Saints* most *preciose is*,
And Hee who helped *David* to bewail
His *Jon'than*, would not my Endeavours fail.
   A sprightly *Effort* of *Poetick Fire*
Would e'en Transport mee to a mad Desire: 45
How could I wish, Oh! that the nimble *Sun*
Of thy short Life before thy Day was done
Might *backward Ten Degrees* have moved! or
Oh! that thy *Corps* might but have chanced for
To have been buried near *Elisha's*[11] bones!   50
Oh! that the Hand which rais'd the *Widows Song*
Would give thee to thy Friends again! But, Fy!
That Passion's vain! To sob, *Why didst thou dy?*
Is but an *Irish Note*: Death won't Restore
His *Stolen Goods* till Time shall be no more.   55
   Shall I take what a *Prologue Homer* hath
Lett mee Relate the Heavenly Powers Wrath?
Or shall I rather join with *Jeremie*,[12]
And o're our great and good *Josiah*[13] sigh,
O that my Head were waters, and mine Eyes   60
A fountain were, that Hadadrimmon's[14] *Cryes*
Might bubble from mee! O that Day and Night

For the Slain of my People weep I might!
Ah! Why delay I? Reader, step with mee,
And what is for thee on *Grief's Table* see   65
Memoria,[15] *Præteritum*[16] is
The *Dish* I call thee to: Come taste of this.
Oakes was! Ah! miserable word! But what
Hee was. Let Never, Never be forgot.
Beleeve mee once, It were a worthy thing   70
Of's *Life* and *Worth* a large Account to bring
To publick *View,* for general *Benefit.*
I would essay (with Leave, Good Reader) it,
So far as *feet* will carry mee; but know it
From first to last, *Grief never made good Poet.*   75
Hee that *lasht* with a *Rod* could *versify,*
Attain'd, and could pretend far more than I!
 Short was thy *Life!* Sweet Saint! & quickly run
Thy *Race!* Thy *Work* was, oh! how quickly done!
Thy *Dayes* were (*David's measure*) but a *Span;*   80
Five Tens of Years roll'd since thy Life began.
Thus I remember a *Greek Poet* Rhimes,
They whom God Loves are wont to dy betimes.
Thus *Whit'ker, Perkins, Preston,*[17] Men of Note,
Ay! many such, Never to *fifty* got.   85
And thus (Rachel New-England!) many Seers
Have left us in the *akme* of their Years.
Good Soul! Thy *Jesus* who did for thee *dy,*
In Heaven longed for thy *Company.*
And let thy *Life* be measur'd by thy *Deeds,*   90
Not by thy *Years;*[18] Thy *Age* strait nothing needs.
Divert, My Pen! Run through the *Zodiac*
Of *Oakes* his *Life:* And cause I knowledge lack
Of most Occurrents, let mee now and then
Snatch at a Passage worthy of a Pen.   95
 Our Mother *England,* ev'n a *Village* there
(*Fuller,*[19] insert it!) did this *Worthy* bear.
Over the *Ocean* in his *Infancy*
His Friends with him into *New-England* fly:
Here, while a lad, almost a *miracle*   100
(As I have heard his Aged Father tell)
Sav'd him from *drowning* in a River: Hee
Would (guess) a *Miracle* and *Moses* bee.
Now did *Sweet Nature* in him so appear
A *Gentlewoman* once cry'd out, *If ere*   105

Good Nature could bring unto Heaven, then
Those wings would thither carry Urian.
Prompt *Parts*, and early *Piety* now made
Men say of him, what once observers said
Of great *John Baptist*, and of *Ambrose*[20] too,   110
To what an one will this strange Infant grow?
Her *Light* and *Cup* did happy *Harvard* give
Unto him; and from her he did receive
His *Two Degrees*: (A double *Honour* to
Thee (*Harvard! Own it!*) did by this accrue!)   115
So being furnisht with due burnisht *Tools*
The *Armour* and the *Treasure* of the *Schools*,
To *Temple-work* he goes: I need not tell
How he an *Hiram*,[21] or *Bezaleel*[22]
Did there approve himself; I'le only add   120
Roxbury[23] his *first-fruits* (*first Sermon*) had.

 Some things invite: Hee back to *England* goes;
With God and Man hee there in favour growes:
But whilst he lives in that Land, *Tichfield*[24] cryes
Come over, Sir, and help us! He complyes: 125
The *Starr* moves thither! There the *Orator*
Continu'd charming sinful mortals for
To close with a sweet Jesus: Oh! he woo'd,
He Thundred: Oh! for their eternal good
How did he bring the *Promises*, and how   130
Did he discharge flashes of *Ebal*?[25] Now
Hee held Love's *golden Scepter* out before
The Humble Soul; Now made the *Trumpet* roar
Fire, Death, and Hell against Impenitent
Desp'rates, untill hee made their hearts relent.   135
There did hee merit *Sibs's*[26] Motto, *I*
Just like a Lamp, with lighting others dy.[27]
Ah! like a *Silk-worm*, his own *bowels* went
To serve his Hearers, while he soundly spent
His *Spirits* in his Labours. O but there   140
He must not dy (except *Death Civil*) Here
(Why mayn't we Sigh it! here) dark *Bartholmew*[28]
This gallant and heroic *Witness* slew.
Silenc't he was! not *buried* out of sight!
A worthy *Gentlemen*[29] do's him invite   145
Unto him; and like *Obadiah*,[30] hide
Him, dear to them with whom he did reside,

Finding his *Prayers* and *Presence* to produce
An *Obed-Edom's*[31] blessing on the House.
A Spirit of great Life from God do's enter   150
Within a while into him: Hee do's venture
To *stand upon* his *feet*: Hee prophesy's;
And to a *Congregation Preacher* is,
Join'd with a loving *Collegue;* who will not
Be buried, till *Symmons*[32] be forgot.   155

But our *New-England-Cambridge* wants him, and
Sighs, *"Of my Sons* none takes me by the hand,
"Now *Mitchel's*[33] gone! Oh! where's his parallel?
"Call my Child *Urian!* Friendly Strangers tell
"An *OAKE* of my own breed in *England* is,   160
"That will support mee Pillar-like; and this
"Must be resolv'd; I'le *Pray* and *Send!* Agreed!
Messengers go! and calling *Council*, speed!
The good *Stork* over the *Atlantic* came.
To nourish and cherish his Aged *Dam.*   165

Welcome! great Prophet! to *New-England* shore!
Thy *feet* are *beautiful!* A number more
Of Men like thee with us would make us say,
The *Moral* of *More's* fam'd *Utopia*[34]
Is in *New-England!* yea, (far greater!) wee   170
Should think wee *Twisse's guess*[35] accomplisht see,
When New Jerusalem comes down, the Seat
Of it, the wast America *will bee't.*
  Cambridge! thy Neighbours must congratulate
Thy Fate! Oh! where can thy *Triumvirate*   175
Meet with its Mate? A *Shephard! Mitchel!* then
An *Oakes!* These *Chrysostoms,*[36] these *golden Men,*
Have made thy *golden Age!* That fate is thine
(To bee blest with the Sun's perpetual Shine)
What *Sylvius*[37] sais of *Rhodes.* Sure thou mayst call   180
Thy Name *Capernaum!*[38] But oh! the *fall*
Of that enlightened Place wee'l humbly pray
Dear Lord! Keep *Cambridge* from it!———
But Quill! where fly'st thou? Let the Reader know
Cambridge some years could this brite *Jewel* show,   185
Yet here a *Quartane Ague*[39] does arrest
The Churches Comfort, & the Countryes Rest.
But this (Praise Mercy) found some *Ague-frighter,*

Hee mends, and his Infirmity grows lighter,
Ev'n that his dear *Orestes*[40] smil'd, *So small*   190
Your Illness, you'd as good have none at all.
Well! the poor Colledge faints! *Harvard* almost
(An *Amnesty* cryes'*st*!) gives up the ghost!
The *branches* dwindle! But an *OAK* so near
May cherish them! 'Twas done! The gloomy fear   195
Of a *lost Colledge* was dispell'd! The Place,
The Learning, the Discretion, and the Grace
Of that *great Charles*,[41] who long since slept & dy'd
Lov'd, and Lamented, worthy *Oakes* supply'd.
His *Nurse* he *suckles;* and the *Ocean* now   200
Refunds what th' *Earth* in *Rivers* did bestow.
Pro Tempore (a sad *Prolepsis*) was
For a long time his *Title;* but just as
Wee had obtain'd a long'd for Alteration,
And fixt him in the *Præsident's* firm Station,   205
The wrath of the Eternal wields a blow
At which my Pen is gastred![42]————

But Up!—Lord! wee're undone!—Nay! Up and Try!
Heart! Vent thy *grief*! Ease *Sorrow* with a *Sigh*!
Lett's hear the matter! Write *de Tristibus*![43]   210
Alas! Enough!————*Death hath bereaved us*!
The *Earth* was parch't with horrid *heat:* We fear'd
The *blasts* of a Vast *Comet's flaming Beard.*
The dreadful *Fire* of Heaven inflames the *blood*
Of our *Elijah,* carrying him to God.   215
Innumerable *Sudden Deaths* abound!
Our *OAKES* a *Sudden blow* laid on the ground,
And gives him blessed *Capel's*[44] wish, which the
Letany prayes 'gainst, *To dy Suddenlie.*
The Saints hope to have the *Lord's Table* Spread;   220
But with astonishment they find him *dead*
That us'd to *break* the *Bread of Life:* O wee
Deprived of our *Ministers* often bee
At such a *Season.* Lord, thy Manna low
In our blind Eyes we fear is wont to go!   225
    The *Man of God* at the first *Touch* do's feel
[With a *Præsage*] his call to Heavens weal;
Hee fits himself for his *last conflict;* Saw
The ghastly *King of Terrors* Icy claw;
Ready to grapple with him; then he gives   230

57

A Look to him who *dy'd and ever lives;*
The great *Redeemer* do's *disarm* the *Snake;*
And by the Hand his faithful *Servant* take,
Leading him thorow *Death's black Valley,* till
Hee brings him in his arms to *Zion's Hill.*   235
Fall'n Pillar of the Church! This Thy Translation
Has turn'd our Joyes into this *Lamentation!*[45]
Sweet Soul! Disdaining any more to *trade*
With *fleshly Organs,* that a *Prison* made,
Thou'rt flown into the *World of Souls,* and wee   240
Poor, stupid Mortals lose thy Companie.
Thou join'st in Consort with the Happy *gone,*
Who (happ'er than *Servants of Solomon*)
Are standing round the Lamb's illustrious Throne
Conversing with great *Isr'el's-Holy-One.*   245
Now could I with good old *Grynæus*[46] say
"Oh! that will be a bright and gloriose Day,
"When I to that Assembly come; and am
"Gone from a world of guilt, filth, sorrow, shame![47]
I read how Swan-like *Cotton* joy'd in Thought,   250
That unto *Dod,*[48] and such he should be brought.
How *Bullinger*[49] deaths grim looks could not fright
Because twould bring him to the *Patriarchs* Sight.
(Well might it be so! *Heathen Socrates*
In hopes of *Homer,* Death undaunted sees.)   255
Who knows but the Third Heaven may sweeter be
Thou *Citizen* of it! (dear *Oakes!*) for thee?
Sure what of *Calvin Beza*[50] said; and, what
Of thy forerunner *Mitchel, Mather* wrote,
I'le truly add, *Now* Oakes *is dead, to mee*   260
Life will less sweet, and Death less bitter bee.
Lord! Lett us follow!——————

Nay! Then, Good Reader! Thou and I must try
To *Tread* his *Steps!* Hee walk't *Exemplar'ly!*
Plato would have none to be prais'd, but those   265
Whose *Praises profitable* wee suppose:
Oh! that I had a *ready Writer's Pen,*
(If not *Briareus*[51] hundred *Hands!*) and then
I might limn forth a *Pattern.* Ah! his own
Fine *Tongue* can his *own worth Describe* alone   270
That's it I want; and poor I! Shan't I show
Like the man, whom *an Hero hired to*

58

Forbear his Verses on him![52] Yet a *lame*
Mephiboshoth[53] will scape a *David*'s blame.

Well! Reader! Wipe thine Eyes! & see the *Man*   275
(Almost too *small* a word!) which *Cambridge* can
Say, I have lost! In N*ame a Drusius,*[54]
And *Nature* too! yea a compendious
Both *Magazine of worth,* and Follower
Of all that ever great and famose were.   280
A *great Soul* in a *little Body.* (Add!
In a small *Nutshell* Graces *Iliad.*)
How many *Angels* on a Needle's point
Can stand, is thought, perhaps, a *needless Point:*
Oakes Vertues too I'me at a loss to tell:[55]   285
In short, *Hee was New-England's SAMUEL;*
And had as many gallant Propertyes
As ere an *Oak* had *Leaves;* or *Argus Eyes.*
A better *Christian* would a *miracle*
Be thought! From most he bore away the *Bell!*   290
Grace and *good Nature* were so purely mett
In him, wee saw in *Gold* a *Jewel* sett.
His very *Name* spake *Heavenly;* and Hee
Vir sui Nominis[56] would alwayes bee.[57]
For a Converse with God; and holy frame,   295
A *Noah,* and an *Enoch* hee became.
Urian and *George* are Names æquivalent;
Wee had *Saint George,* though other Places han't.
Should I say more, like him that would extol
Huge *Hercules,* my Reader'l on me fall   300
With such a check; *Who does dispraise him?* I
Shall say enough, if his *Humility*
Might be described. Witty *Austin*[58] meant
This is the *First, Second,* and *Third* Ornament,
Of a Right Soul, should be esteem'd. And so   305
Our *Second Moses,*[59] Humble *Dod,* cry'd, *Know,*
Just as Humility mens Grace will bee,
And so much Grace so much Humilitie.
Ah! *graciose Oakes,* wee saw thee *stoop;* wee saw
In thee the *Moral* of good *Nature*'s *Law,*   310
That the *full Ears* of *Corn* should *bend,* and grow
Down to the ground: *Worth would sit alwayes low.*
    And for a *Gospel Minister,* wee had
In him a *Pattern* for our *Tyro's;*[60] Sad!

Their Head is gone: Who ever knew a greater 315
Student and *Scholar?* or beheld a better
Preacher and *Præsident?* Wee look't on him
As *Jerom* in our (Hungry) *Bethlechem;*
A perfect *Critic* in *Philology;*
And in *Theology* a *Canaan's Spy.* 320
His *Gen'ral Learning* had no fewer *Parts*
Than the *Encyclopædia of Arts:*
The old Say, *Hee that something is in all,*[61]
Nothing's in any; Now goes to the wall.
But when the *Pulpit* had him! there hee spent 325
Himself as in his onely *Element:*
And there hee was an *Orpheus:*[62] Hee'd e'en draw
The *Stones,* and *Trees: Austin* cryes, *If I saw*
Paul in the Pulpit, of my Three Desires
None of the least (to which my Soul aspires) 330
Would gratify'd and granted bee. Hee might
Have come and seen't, when *OAKES* gave Cambridge Light.
Oakes an *Uncomfortable Preacher* was
I must confess! Hee made us cry, *Alass!*
In sad *Despair!* Of what? Of *ever seeing* 335
A better Preacher while wee have a beeing.
Hee! oh! *Hee* was, in *Doctrine, Life,* and all
Angelical, and *Evangelical.*
A *Benedict* and *Boniface* to boot,
Commending of the *Tree* by noble *Fruit.* 340
All said, Our *Oakes* the *Double Power* has
Of *Boanerges,*[63] and of *Barnabas:*[64]
Hee is a *Christian Nestor!*[65] Oh! that wee
Might him among us for *three Ages see!*
But ah! Hee's gone to *Sinus Abrahæ.*[66] 345
What shall I say? Never did any spitt
Gall at this *Gall-less, Guile-less Dove;* nor yet
Did any *Envy* with a cankred breath
Blast him: It was I'me sure the gen'ral Faith,
Lett Oakes *Bee, Say,* or *Do* what e're he wou'd, 350
If it were *OAKES,* it must be *wise, true, good.*
Except the *Sect'ryes Hammer* might a blow
Or two, receive from *Anabaptists,* who
Never lov'd any Man, that wrote a Line
Their naught, Church-rending Cause to undermine. 355
Yett after my *Encomiastick Ink*
Is all run out, I must conclude (I think)
With a *Dicebam,*[67] not a *Dixi!* Yea,[68]

60

Such a course will exceeding proper bee:
The *Jews*, whene're they build an *House*, do leave   360
Some *part Imperfect*, as a call to *grieve*
For their *destroy'd Jerus'lem*! I'le do so!
I do't!————————————————

And now let *sable Cambridge* broach her Tears!
(They *forfeit* their own *Eyes* that don't; for
                              (here's   365
Occasion sad enough!) Your *Sons* pray call
All *Ichabod*;[69] and *Daughters, Marah*![70] Fall
Down into Sack-cloth, Dust, and Ashes! (To
Bee senseless Now, Friends, Now! will be to show
A *CRIME & BADG*[71] of *Sin* and *Folly*!) *Try*   370
Your *fruitfulness* under the Ministry
Of that kind *Pelican*, who spent his *Blood*
To feed you! Dear *Saints*! Have ye got the Good
You might? And let a *Verse* too *find* the Men
Who *fly'd a Sermon*! Oh! Remember when   375
Sirs! Your *Ezekiel* was like unto
A *lovely Song of* (Been't *deaf Adders* you)
One with a pleasant Voice! and that could play
Well on an Instrument! And i'n't the Day,
The *gloriose* Day, to dawn (ah! yet!) wherein   380
You are drawn from the *Egypt-graves* of *Sin*
Compelled to come in? *For shame come in!*
Nay! Join you all! *Strive* with a *noble Strife*,
To *publish* both in *Print* (as well as *Life*)
Your preciose Pastor's *Works*! Bring them to view   385
That wee may *Honey* tast, as well as you.
But, Lord! What has thy *Vineyard* done, that thou
Command'st the *Clouds* to rain no more? O shew
Thy favour to thy *Candlestick*! Thy *Rod*
Hath almost broke it: Lett a *Gift of God*,   390
Or a sincerely Heaven-touch't *Israelite*
Become a *Teacher* in thy Peoples sight.

   At last I with *License Poetical*
(Reader! and thy good leave) address to all
The children of thy People! Oh! the *Name*   395
Of *Urian Oakes*, New-England! does proclame
SURE I AN OAK[72] was to thee! Feel thy Loss!
Cry, (*Why forsaken, Lord!*) Under the Cross!
Learn for to *prize Survivers*! *Kings destroy*

The People that *Embassadors* annoy.   400
The Counsil of God's *Herald,* and thy *Friend,*
[*Bee wise! Consider well thy latter End!*][73]
O lay to heart! Pray to the heavenly *Lord*
Of th' Harvest, that (according to his Word)
Hee would *thrust forth his Labourers:* For why   405
Should all thy *Glory* go, and *Beauty dy*
Through thy default?————————
————————Lord! from they lofty Throne
Look down upon thy *Heritage!* Lett none
Of all our *Breaches* bee unhealed! Lett   410
This dear, poor Land be our *Immanuel's*[74] yett!
Lett's bee a *Goshen*[75] still! Restrain the Boar
That makes *Incursions!* Give us daily more
Of thy All-curing *Spirit* from on High!
Lett all thy *Churches* flourish! And supply   415
The almost *Twenty Ones,* that thy Just Ire
Has left *without Help* that their Needs require!
Lett not the *Colledge* droop, and dy! O Lett
The Fountain run! A *Doctor* give to it!
Moses's are to th' *upper Canaan* gone!   420
Lett *Joshua*'s Succeed them! goes when one
Elijah, raise *Elisha's! Pauls* become
Dissolv'd! with Christ! Send *Tim'thees* in their room!
Avert the *Omen,* that when *Teeth* apace
Fall out, No *new ones* should supply their place!   425

    Lord! Lett us *Peace* on this our *Israel* see!
And still both *Hephsibah,*[76] and *Beulah* bee![77]
Then will thy People *Grace!* and *Glory!* Sing,
And every Wood with *Hallelujah's* ring.

                    N. R.

Vixere fortes ante Agamemnona
Multi; sed illachrymabiles
Urgentur ignotiq; longa
Nocte; carent quia Vate sacro.   Hor.

Non ego cuncta meis amplecti Versibus opto.   Virg.

————————Ingens laudato Poema:
Exiguum legito!————   Call.

Qui legis ista, tuam reprehendo si mea laudes
Omnia, Stultitiam: Si nihil, Invidiam.   Owen.

Non possunt, Lector, multae emendare Lituræ
  Versus hos nostros: Una Litura potest.   Martial.[78]

AN
ELEGY
ON The Much-to-be-deplored DEATH
OF *That Never-to-be-forgotten PERSON,*

The Reverend
Mr. *NATHANAEL COLLINS;*[1]

Who After he had been many years a *faithful*
Pastor to the Church at *Middletown* of
Connecticut in *New-England,*
about the *Forty third* year of his Age Expired;
On 28*th*. 10. *moneth* 1684.

FUNERAL-TEARS

At the Grave of the much *Desired*
And *Lamented*
Mr. NATHANEEL COLLINS,
Who changed Death for *LIFE,*
December 28. 1684.

—But shall he unobserved steal away?
Or *Israel* not afford an *hand* to lay[2]
An Evil-boding *Death* to *heart*? no Son
Of All the Prophets when *Elijah's* gone
Look after him?   5

Forbid this, Heaven! *Showr*
On a bereaved Clod *of Earth a pow'r*
To yield a spire of grass[3] *whereon may grow*
The Name of COLLINS, *help a verse to show*
His *Vertues, as that* Flock *acknowledged*   10
Their Doe[4] *when to the Spicy* Mountains *fled.*
Assist mee, thou who hast engag'd the Just
A Memory,[5] *to whom the precious dust*
Of Saints Dissolv'd *remains* united!—

   I SIGH the *Fate* for which our broached eyes   15
Spend floods of *brine;* at which a dire surprise
Of a soul-chilling horrour doth invade
The *Soul* not *stone* before; at which are made
In serious minds as many *wounds* as were
To *Caesar*[6] given. Reader, shake to hear: 20

The DEATH of COLLINS tis. He dead without
A *Paper* winding sheet to lay him out!
A Shame. O that *Egyptian Odours,* and
Embalmers too[7] were not at my command!
I want them. But *Hyperboles* withdraw,   25
Be gone *Licentious Poets.* What I saw
On this occasion let some countrey Rymes
That call a Spade a *Spade,* tell after-Times.
   DEPRIV'D of *Charrets & of Horsmen* too,[8]
I on the wings of *Contemplation* flew;   30
Into the howling *desart* thus I went,
The *cut-off garden*[9] where our *David* sent
His *sheep* to feed and fold, from which he drave
The Rav'nous *Tigre-brood,* in which he gave
His herds a *Rest at noon.*[10] On *Jordans* Banks   35
I meant to sit with *Thoughts* on this and *Thanks.*
But there found I an *Elect Lady,*[11] There
Grov'ling in Ashes, with dishev'led hair,
Smiting her breast, *black'd* with a *mourning* dress,
Resembling mother *Sion in distress;*[12]   40
Or like a *Rachel* in a *Bethl'em* plight,[13]
But with a *Beauty* glittering too, that might
The Features show that Judah's *preaching King*
Much did once in his machless Raptures sing;[14]
I found her. There amaz'd, into a *Tree*[15]   45
Almost transformed with passion: *Sympathie*

64

Produced this Enquiry, *Who I wonder,*
Seems Sorrow's Center, *Sorrow's* Essence yonder?
Lo, I no sooner had approached near,
Then from above this voice did thunder; *Here*   50
Pitty, the Church of Middletown *bespeaks*
Set in the midst of *swoons and sobs and shrieks.*
With Bowells full of *it* I hastned to
The *Wet place,* asking *Why she grieved so;*
And had this Answer.   55

Sir, *Ask* you this? Are you a Sojourner
    Within *New-Englands* bounds & know not *why?*
I've lost great *COLLINS,* man! O that, O there,
    From *this Tears-Fountain*[16] is my misery.

Immortal COLLINS! what a *Charm* is in   60
    So dear a *Name?* 'Tis *Honey* mixt with *gall*
To think, I *had* him, but I *miss* him; Seen
    He *was,* sad word![17] but so *no* more *be shall.*

My *love* is Talkative: tis fit that I
    Thus vent my *smother'd Fire.* The *Rabbins* say   65
That when good old *Methusela* did dye,
    His Wife *nine husbands* lost in him that day.

Like *Looser*[18] I will *speak:* The *Lamentation*
    Over Jerus'lems *Woe* doth suit me *well,*
A Widow how is she become![19] Privation   70
    Seems now to be my only *Principle.*

Once did I *prise,* I'l now *praise* what I had.
    The *box* of his Fames *Oyntment*[20] now shall send
Abroad its Odours. *Alexander*[21] dead
    Had not the *scent* which doth from him ascend.   75

Some *Elogyes* compose to try their Wits;
    The *Gout,*[22] the *Feavour,*[23] yea & *Injustice,*[24]
Folly[25] and *Poverty*[26] have in the Fits
    Of Ranting Writers had a *comeliness.*

My *Theme,* my *Humour* is not such an one: 80
    Who to prove *Cicero* not eloquent,
Pen'd Books,[27] who *truth & worth* for *guards* disown
    Such only count *Collins not excellent.*

Bright COLLINS, Star of the *first Magnitude*,
    Extol him how could I! I sha'n't be chid   85
If as much time on him my *gazes* shou'd
    Spend, as that *Greek*[28] in's *Panegyric* did.

O that *Apelles*[29] were my servant now
    To *limn* this *Hero*, but his utmost *All*
Would blush, and draw a *vail* upon the Brow[30]   90
    Below whose *Majesty* his *skill* would fall.

I would that you, my Friend, each *drop* of Ink
    Could fill with *Elogyes* no fewer then
The little *eels*[31] that may swim in't: I think
    They all should celebrate this *Flow'r of men*.   95

I would too that each *syllable* all round
    This Globe with *perfum'd Air* might fly about;
Or your *Stentorophonic Tube*[32] might found
    The praise of admirable *Collins* out.

Death, thou *All-biting*[33] *Prodigall*, a blow   100
    Of thine hath laid *within* the ground a plant
Surpassing *Cedars*. I did hardly know
    A *spice* whose quantity on *it* was scant.

Good *Nature and* good *Education* were
    In him conjoyn'd to such an high degree,   105
As gain'd the Title of that[34] *Emperour*,
    In this rare soul *Mankinds delight* we see.

Facetious Snow-balls from his candid breast
    With early Magic hence would captivate
His near, Familiars, so that he was blest   110
    Who could have leave to be his Intimate.

Hence from his Cradle clothes his neat *discretion*,
    Mounted upon bridled *Urbanity*,
Before a most obliging *Disposition*,
    Triumphant rode in ev'ry *Company*.   115

But Oh the *fruits* of Heav'nly *Graces* dew
    Upon so rich a *soyl!* Let *Peter* bid
His *Brethren* add one graces *pearl* unto
    The[35] rest; The whole *heap* was in *Collins* hid.

You'd scarce believe the FAITH residing in 120
    This Child of *Abraham*, the strong Impression
On his heart of *Realities* unseen,[36]
    Of *Gospel glories*, of things past expression:

How dearest to him his *Redeemer*; how
    With brave *Ignatius*[37] he could warble out 125
O Christ my Love; how we might e'en allow
    A *JESUS* grav'd[38] within his breast no doubt.

His VERTUE took this *sister* by the hand;
    And with her *train* accompanyed thus,
In *vert'ous flights* he went—how much beyond 130
    An *Aristides*;[39] or a *Regulus*![40]

For KNOWLEDGE, tho in him poor *Harvard* lost
    One of her *tallest sons*, one of the best
Souldiers in her *Minerva*'s Camp, my boast
    Of *higher Wisdom* in him i'n't the least. 135

My *Moses*, he in *Egypts Learning* verst[41]
    Had more then *that*; Accomplishments *Divine*
In exercise of which, while he converst
    With Isr'els Jah, to us his face did shine.[42]

Yare at his GRAMMAR, kenning *how* and *when* 140
    To speak: his *tongue* a[43] *tree of life*, no (dross
Proceeding from this *Chrysostom*)[44] the *penn*
    Of *Ready writers* like, not *barbarous*.

How *lofty* in his RHET'RIC, when with cryes
    To the Omnipotent reduc'd to say[45] 145
Let me alone, thereby he scal'd the Skyes,
    And with the old[46] *Artill'ry* got the day.

In the best LOGIC, Oh how *Rational*!
    How able to spy *Canaan* through! how ready
To baffle a *Temptation*! and withal 150
    Full of his *Oracles* sound, solid, steady!

How right was his ARITHMETIC that knew
    Wisely to measure his own[47] *dayes*! How right
Was his GEOMETRY, that found the true
    Bulk of the *earth*! a point[48] not worth the *sight*. 155

In his ASTRONOMY how ripe his eye
  Reaching to things beyond the *stars*! Alwayes
Exact in this *no-vain*[49] PHILOSOPHY,
  That in all things he found his *Makers*[50] *praise.*

Master of all the *Arts* that shew us what   160
  Tis from each *Bad* unto each *Good* to goe;
To all his *Knowledge* last subjoyning *that*,[51]
  All that I know is, that I nothing know.

For TEMPERANCE, he liv'd upon it, hee
  Like *Hooper* spar'd much in his *diet*, more   165
In 's *speech*, but most in *Time*; the hateful *Three*
  Fly-gods[52] o' the' world mean while he car'd not for.

To *Meat* a[53] *Daniel*; and a *Rechabite*[54]
  To *Drink*; like a *John Baptist*[55] in his *Rayment*;
His *sleep*, like *David*,[56] robbing in the Night;   170
  Still putting *Nature* off with *scanty payment.*

Abstemious in all things·at such a rate,
  Some (like *Eliza*[57] in her *Brothers* eyes,
Him *Brother Temp'rance* could denominate.
  And *Justice* caus'd what e'er lookt otherwise.   175

For PATIENCE whole *beds* and *loads* of it
  In his soul flourisht. What *Affliction* meant
He *felt* as much as most do *talk*, and yet
  Groans might from him, but *Grumbles*[58] ne're be sent.

And under *Provocation*, 'twas a care   180
  By him maintaind to *smile Affronts away.*
Not fireing when meer *Cock-boats* landed are,
  Seldom decoy'd from his mild *Yea,* or *Nay.*

No Brother of *Achilles;*[59] like unto
  The *Upper Regions* free from Tempests; full   185
Of the *doves temper:* Able for to go
  Over an *Alphabet,*[60] tho *Anger* pull.

His GODLINESS *steer'd*[61] all his motions still:
  God had his *thrice-hot*[62] *love*, his life, his Whole:
Gods *Honour* was his End, *and* in the *Will*   190
  Of God he *moulded*[63] his renewed soul.

68

His sev'rall *Turns* on a Religious *threed*
   He sought to string: fixing that *Motto* on
What signal he in both his *Callings* did,
   With much devotion, *Lord*[64] *for thee alone.*   195

How *James*-like were his[65] *Pray'rs*, how did the *word*
   Of Life, his heart *Christs*[66] *Library* affect!
What God-ward flames did his *pure*[67] *mind* afford
   Of any *Ord'nance* dreading a Neglect!

BROTHERLY-KINDNESS did procure the *Law*   200
   Of Kindness in his[68] *lips,* a Denison
Of *Philædelphia*[69] in him we saw;
   Heir to the soul of the Apostle[70] *John.*

A *Zwinglian* entire that ever said[71]
   Let me see Christ *in anyone, I shall*   205
Him with both Armes embrace. Whatever made
   Distinctions, this with him removed all.

And CHARITY in him *warm Beams* extended
   To all the Race of Man; *Philanthropy*
Him like a *shaddow* every where attended;   210
   COLLINS made up of Love, we us'd to cry.

An *Injury* seldom resenting more
   Than *Cranmer*[72] or the *Martyrologer*[73]
Who *urn'd* his *Ashes,* of whom tis notour,
   Of good, for ill, Turns from them sure you were.   215

In fine, As the[74] *Philosopher* did give
   His friend advice, *suppose a* Cato's *eye*[75]
On you, and so be wise; when I would live
   Uprightly, I'd imagine *COLLINS* by.

Thus was he for a *Christian,* and thus he   220
   With Conversation *lightned,* every *Deed*
Of his in print a *Sermon* yeeldeth mee:[76]
   But now what as a *Minister* you'l heed.

Methinks I see how fraught the *Pulpit* was
Of Grace, of Gravity, of Wisdom, when   225
With most harmonious notes a *Barnabas*[77]
   He now was, and a *Boanerges*[78] then:

69

How *deep* his Sermons were, where *Elephants*
    Might take content, and yet withal how plain,
Suited unto the *leather Dublet's* Wants.   230
    All in a near unimitable Strain:

What *undasht*[79] *wine* he gave me: what a *Zeal*
    For me consum'd him: how *material*
He was in *Dispensations* aim'd to heal
    Distempers in me, yet how *Spiritual:*   235

He like an *Ox* was alwaies labouring
    To feed me, but he like an *Eagle*[80] too
Did soar to *Pisgah's* Top,[81] from thence to bring
    Celestial *Visions* pore-blind us unto.

One is a *Doctor* most[82] *Invincible*   240
    Another most[83] *Profound,* a Third is counted
A *Subtil*[84] one; (Scholastic Records tell)
    A Fourth[85] *Angelical* by none surmounted:

COLLINS was *all* of this. The noble[86] *Three*
    Geneva Crowns, enlightening *Calvin,* and   245
The thundring *Farel*[87] join' auspiciouslie
    With shouring *Viret,*[88] here in one did stand.

For *Memory* almost a *Seneca,*[89]
    For *Judgement* and *Fancy* inferior
To few: in Learning rich, and ev'ry way   250
    He was a *furnisht* Gospel-Orator.

How many[90] *Lydian*-hearts reputed him
    A *Claviger,*[91] by him *unlocked*? To us
For *Light* giv'n to our *House* how much Esteem
    He had as an[92] *Oecolampadius!*[93]   255

To save poor me and mine, Oh how *severe*[94]
    His *Labours* were! how lasting his Renown
Must to my *Offspring* be, *Once* (saying) *were*
    Doves eyes within the Locks of[95] Middletown!

My *Neighbourhood* shar'd with me too; he gave   260
    Some *Spirit* unto them: and then his[96] *Haven*
He chose: So on the *Day*[97] we us'd to have
    Heaven from *him,* from *us he* flew to *Heaven.*

The Age of *Perkins*[98] just attaind, he thought
   It time to follow him. But *Why so fast?*   265
The *cause* you know that of *such things* is brought
   Belong'd to him, *he only grew too fast.*[99]

More would I say but Heart-corroding *Anguish*
   Layes that check on me, *you have lost him now.*
Broken with thy big Loss dear Friend, I languish.   270
   Hence would my *Tears* more than my *River* flow.

Now in *Micaiahs*[100] Trance[101] I seem to see
   For *Food* on mountains, wandring Shepherdless,
And Shiftless rambling, what belongs to me.
   Wast *Park* of mine that now no *Keeper* has!   275

Lord, is my *Night* come shall *Impenitent*
   Transgressours now continue *so?* Shall it
Upon my *Meeting-House,* while men repent,
   This and that man born here[102] no more be writ?

Shall a forsaken now *Society*   280
   Without its *Head*, its *Heart*, its *Eyes* remain?
And like *Isaiah*'s woful *Vineyard* ly[103]
   With with'ring *Grapes* abandon'd by the *Rain?*

O Ghastly *Omens!* if *Paræus*[104] dy
   Let *Heidleberge*[105] look to't. If *Austin* go   285
Let *Hippo*[106] tremble. If *Elisha* fly[107]
   After his Master, *next year* brings a wo.

I fear of both sorts now[108] *Mortalities,*
   Of *Famines* too I fear the[109] worst, I fear
The *Gallop* of no less Calamities   290
   Then can be wrap'd in a pale *Comets* Hair.

Amidst these hideous *Frights* perplext, I mourn
   With *Incohærent* Throbs you see. Now tell me
Whether it be not *just* that thus forlorn
   I here bewail this that has late befel me.   295

   SHE said; Her heavy words were hardly out
When, as one *planet-struck,* a doleful shout
Of the surviving COLLINSes detaind
Me from *Replies* to what had been complain'd.

To fill the *Stage* there seem'd to throng a croud   300
Of his *Relations* to us. First aloud
His Aged *Parents* with drench'd Hankerchiefs
Saw and *had* cause thus to proclaim their Griefs:

   A *Son, our* Staff and[110] Stork; (said they) *A Son,*
Our Benjamin, *Alas, must* he *be gone*   305
To his Long-Home *before us? Heaven more*
May now be Heaven *to us than before.*

Farewel, thou world of[111] Dirt; *we meekly wait*
But for a[112] *Call too.* This deplored: Straight
His *Brethren* not as a[113] *Jehoiakim*[114]   310
But as a[115] *Jonathan,* bemoaned him,
With this, *We live to see the* Joseph *die,*
Whom we thought born for our Adversity!

   His *Widdow* then, (the tender *Whiting* swam
Thro' the *Black*[116] *sea of Death* to us) *I came*   315
(Said She) *to bear a part with you. But I*
Must in deep Silence *do't. That ev'ry Sigh*
Of mine—O that it Marbles *might erect*
To him, *for lack of* whom *I'm thus deject.*

   And then his *Orphans,* all *ensabled* add   320
O could be say—that once a Father had,
A Father whose paternal over-sight
Did make us over happy, whose Delight
Was in our Welfare, *whose Behaviours*
*Still taught us—*Mercy! *what a loss is our's!*

   In this Distraction *mixing* once again
A *Consolation-cup;*[117] Thick *Mists* amain
About us gathering; a Murmur there
Of the *blest Shade* himself we then might hear.

FOND *Mortals;* wipe your eyes (said he) pray keep   330
   That *liquor* for your selves. [118]poor *Envy* 'tis
Which prompts your *Threnodies* for me. To weep
   For *my Sake,* is but to Ignore *my Bliss.*

O what a world of *smoke* of *dust* of *Folly*
   Am I *sayl'd*[119] from! No *sin* shall me annoy,   335

And no *Temptation* more to be *unholy*
    Shall e'er molest me in my *Masters JOY.*

I have my *Ragged mantle* dropt; I have
    All *Vanity* and all *Vexation*[120]
Escap'd, my *Clay* safe kept within a Grave   340
    Preserv'd lies for the *Resurrection.*

No *Cross*[121] shall ever gall my shoulders more,
    From *God*, correcting my *disorders*, and
No *Club e're* strike me, red with ancient Gore,
    Still by each *Cain*[122] retained in his hand.   345

I'm got within the *Vail*, and there I see
    The ever-glorious Face of the[123] GOD-MAN;
And He with Transports doth convey to me
    As much of GOD as entertain I can.

I *Know*, I *Live*, I *Love*; But *How*? forbear   350
    To be inquisitive: It can't be told
To *you*; No, tho you all[124] *Hebricians*[125] were:
    Nor can *shell-vessels*[126] this things meaning hold.

I find besides my loving *Guardians* here,
    Here the *Good Angels* that convey'd me thro'   355
The *Divel-haunted-Dungeon-Atmosphere*,[127]
    To mine annext their *Hallelujahs* do.

Here, me the *Chorus* of the *glorify'd*,
    The *polisht*[128] stones, now in the Temple plac't
The *twice cloath'd*[129] Souls, salute on ev'ry side;   360
    I see *Nathaneel*[130] here, I know the rest.

Be *glad* that I am here, and after hye,
    Your selves with diligence, all *posting* hither,
Precepts and *Patterns* left, my *Counsels* eye,
    And *Copyes*, so we shall be soon together.[131]   365

Souls, follow me. Anon the *Stars*, the *Sands*.
    The *Atoms* of the Universe—a Scrol
Like Heaven fill'd with *Nines*, for *cypher* stands,
    Compar'd to the *Long joyes*[132] that over us may roll.

A *PERIOD* this puts to the *Tragedy.*   370
He vanisht; *They* retir'd; confused I
Now quite *alone*, have nothing else to do,
But to pour out a short *Hosannah* to
The Worlds Almighty GOVERNOUR to where
On this account now these *Petitions* come   375
From lifted *Hands*, and bended *Knees*—
                              Dread Lord,
By whom vast hosts of Beings with a Word
Are made and mov'd: Let they much-hop'd Salvation
Shield us, like Walls from much-fear'd Desolation.   380
O Save New-Englands *Churches; Let them be*
Still golden Candlesticks, belov'd by thee,
Still Puritans; *Still* Iv'ry Pallaces.
Keep up the Quickset Hedge *about them; Please*
To keep the gladsome Streams *of them alive.*   385
Save Middletown, *and cause the Place to thrive*
Under Fat Clouds *still, and that* Bochim *let*
By thy Provision be a Bethel *yet.*
Save ev'ry soul that reads this Elegy;
Like COLLINS *let us live, like* COLLINS *dy.*   390
                    AMEN.
         Sic mihi contingat vivere sicque mori.
                              Sic optat,
         Qui longe sequitur vestigia semper adorans.
                    Qualis vita, ita.[133]

An ELEGY
Upon the DEATH of
Mrs. MARY BROWN;
Who Dyed in Travail,
(with her Unborn Child;) On *Dec.* 26. 1703.[1]
Ætatis Suæ 35.

Monopolizing HEE's, pretend no more
Of *Wit* and *Worth*, to Hoard up all the store.
The *Females* too grow *Wise & Good & Great;*
Some such in happy *Salem* find a Seat.
Beware, *my Sex*, lest *Females* Win the Day,   5

And Shame Us with reviv'd *Hybristica*.[2]
Plutarch,[3] Return to Life, and Write agen,
Of Womens Virtues, to *Upbraid* the Men.

When *Vertuous Women* are in Books Enroll'd,
Let our bright MARY's Name and Fate be told. 10
Of *Glorious Women*, O Great *Hottinger*,[4]
In thy brave *Catalogue*, make Room for *her*.
America thanks *Europe*, and does boast
Her sending such a *Gem* unto our Coast.

Come hither, You that the fair Sex reproach; 15
Confuted now, no more your Scandals broach.
ONE rescues here the Fame of *all* the Sex;
And will your *Contradicted Envy* Vex.
With no *Sett-Offs*, but *Truth* in every *Line*,
We do *Delineate* our *Heroine*. 20
Grammar makes TRUTH, a SHEE; we shall with care
Nothing but very *Truth* of *Her* declare.

TRUTH, Thou shalt be my *Muse*, and first relate
How MARY *Shone* first in her *Virgin-State*.
To *Learn* or *Do* some *Good* thing every Day 25
Was the Prime Study of this *Agatha*.[5]
Ambitious Early to Enjoy a *Mind*,
From Earth, and Foggy Ignorance *refin'd*.
A *Bible*, not *Romance*, her Eyes before,
Then daily help'd her Heaven to implore. 30
Tutors one never more obedient saw;
Their *Word*, their very *Look*, She made her *Law*.
To fill her Soul with high Attainments, Shee
Gladly Out-Labour'd the Industrious *Bee*.
No *Hind Let Loose*; but Guarded well, and grave; 35
Most *Goodly Words*, yet our *Eulalia*[6] gave.
Not *Confident*; Like Damsels which their *Chin*.
Contrive more than their *Tongue*, to *Bridle* in.
Not of the *Gadding Tribe*; nor could She bear,
So Chast! the least Indecent Thing to hear. 40
With still a *Silent Blush*, her Rising Blood
Spoke in her Face, *Care to be very Good*.
Pale with the Fear of doing ill, and *Red*
With Modesty, was all the *Paint* She had.
Go on, dear TRUTH, charge once *Truth-Speaking Fame* 45

75

To Tell *whose Wife,* & *What* She then became.
  BROWN to the *Lottery of Worth* drew near;
He drew a *Prize,* a matchless *Prize,* in *Her.*
Not *Wealth,* but Solid *Worth,* in her he sees;
He see's *Rich Vertues,* and is charm'd with these.   50

    O *Parents,* Pity the fond *Sons* of Men,
    And your fair *Daughters* well adorn for them.
    With *Useful Knowledge* fraight their Tender Souls;
    Why should they *Empty* be, but *Noisy Fools?*
    Teach them the Skill an House to *Guide* & *Feed,*   55
    And with Kind Mates and *Easy* Life to Lead.
    Goodness to them, and all *Good Humour* Show;
    The Pious Parents Shap'd their MARY so.
        The Wretch that is alone to *Mammon*[7] Wed,
    May chance to find a *Satan* in the Bed.   60
    She's Rich! That's all they say on her behalf:
    Her *Gold* you Worship, and a *Golden Calf.*
    Wink hard and Wed; a *Bag* and *Baggage* too,
    In *Markets* often do together go.
    Who by meer *Hundreds* and by *Thousands* choose,   65
    A *Thousand tis to One,* themselves they loose.
    The *Rigging* of the Ship; the Tear & Wear,
    Will soon cost more than all She brought with her.
    Why should her *Dress* Ensnare? Tis dearly bought:
    Poor *Woodcocks* that are in a *Ribbon* caught.   70
    Or why her *Dance* bewitch? Upon an head
    Not like *John Baptists,* her *Light Feet* shall tread.

BROWN Steer'd not so; He ask'd, *A Vertuous Wife,*
The *Soul,* and *Salt,* and Joy of Humane Life.
A Vertuous Wife, Heav'n did on BROWN bestow;   75
So Heav'n Rewards its *Favourites* below.
A *Wife* indeed! Which now so few attain,
Some are so; and thou MARY in the *Van.*
Happy the *Women* were, and Happy too
The *Husbands,* if the Sex were more like YOU.   80
Oh! Would they *Carriage* from your *Conduct* learn;
Be Neat; but make their *Soul,* their main concern.
    Her BROWN, how did She Love, & please & prize;
And *Saw none* but that *Covering of her Eyes!*
The Persian Law, She would not *Alter* too,   85
That Wives give to their Husbands Honour due.
Blame not the *Rabbi's* now for what they Write,

How Heav'n did *Adam* and *Eve*, at first Unite.
Two Bodies then if Heav'n in *One* did frame,
Two Souls here met in *One* united Flame.   90
   Sir, Tho' you *Cloath'd* her as you *Lov'd* her, well,
She would of *You*, more than her *Cloathing* tell.
So *Philo's* Wife,[8] with mean Array Content,
Her Husbands Worth, call'd *Her best Ornament*.
Had you been *Lame*, She'd been the *Herpine*,[9] who   95
In Arms a Thousand Miles had carried You.
Or had it been your Hap to first Expire,
She had felt more than *Portia's*[10] Coals of Fire.
When did She ever once your Patience try,
Or make an *Head-Ake in the Family*!   100
   Yes, Once at Last; She did your Love offend;
T'was by her *Death;* but never, Sir, till *then*!
   Martyr of Love to You, Lov'd *Rachel* Dyed;
And what must now dear BENJAMIN betide?
How many means black *Death* at once to kill?   105
She felt *Two Death's*, and YOU a *Thousand* feel.
   BROWN and his Bride with *Vertuous Love* display
How *Christ* does *Love*, and how his *Church obey*.
   Why did'st thou Father *Jerom*, say, *that Strife*
Must be Essential to the Married Life?   110
Here was a pair, the only *Strife* of whom
Was who should in their *Goodness* overcome.

   Oh come, *Tertullian;*[11] Teach me to declare,
The *Happiness* of such an *Happy Pair*!
Ye *Popish Dogs*, At *Marriage* bark no more;   115
Unclean so *Devils burn*, and *Single* Roar.
Marriage, That *Honourable Chastity*,
Let none but Filthy *Antichrist* decry.

But tell, fair TRUTH; for thou hast more to tell:
What MARY was; Not, where's a *Parallel*!   120
   Her *Beauty* let *Agrippa's* Pen[12] define:
Call it, *A Lovely Ray of Light Divine;*
A *Soul* of *Heav'nly Lustre* Shining thro'
An *Earthly Lanthorn* of a Glorious hue.
A *Body* of a Frame so *fine* and *Rare*,   125

When was there *Matter* seen to *Thought* so near?
   (So *Fair;* but not Enslav'd unto the *Smoke*
   Pip'd by the Dames under the *Indian Yoke!*)

77

But NOYES,[13] except Thou do a *Pencil* find,
None can Paint out the *Beauty* of her *Mind*.   130
Unbodied Vertue She; The *Spangled Sphere*
Look'd for her, and such Lustre must be *there*.
A *Patch'd* Face could not suit so *sound an Heart*,
Spotts to the *Skin* clear Souls do not impart.
Sincere; She *Paint* abhorr'd; a *Jezabel*   135
May *Paint*, but *Meat* unto the *Doggs* she fell.
    Prudence[14] the *Mother* of all Vertues here,
Before She was a *Mother* came to Her.
The Harmless *Dove* nothing of *Serpent* had,
But *Prudence* for to serve and help her *Head*.   140
    By the *Polestar* of *Piety* She Steer'd;
And no mishaps but those of *Sin* She fear'd.
When JESUS call'd, His Mary came to Him,
Clasping the *Feet* that came her to Redeem.
With *Tears* to Channels of *Repentance* turn'd,   145
Faults known to none but *Heav'n & Her*, She mourn'd.
And yet these Lovely Pearls, her Tears, She thought
Must to her Saviours Cleansing Blood be brought.
The Worlds base Idols, her brave Soul despis'd
And what the World Adores She *Sacrific'd*.   150
CHRIST ask'd the *Heart* of Her for whom He dy'd;
Great LORD, *I'm thine!* Her conquer'd Heart reply'd.
His *Righteousness alone* She chose for that
Wherein to Stand before His Judgment Seat:
To that Kind *Shepherd*, gladly She Resign'd   155
To *Lead* and *Rule* by Grace her *Lamb-like* Mind.
    Her Hands to God oft Lift in fervent *Prayer*,
(Hands in Redeeming *Blood* well *Whit'ned*) were.
    When the rare Pastors had their *Sermons done*,
Her *Doing* was, the *Repetition*.   160
    Banquets not in the *Hall*, but at the Door
She still preferr'd, there for to feed the *Poor*.
Her *old Cloaths*, on the *Poor*, a Neater Shew
She judg'd, they made than on *her Self* her *New*.

    Ye Writers on the *Decalogue*,[15] Stand by;   165
Durham[16] and all the rest, shall Needless ly:
The *Life* we saw our pious MARY Live,
A Commentary to the Life, did give.
    But Oh! the *Fourth!*—Tell, How She *Sabbatiz'd;*
And how the *Rapt'rous Day* She spent and priz'd.   170

The *Day of God*, which all our other Dayes
As worth Ten Thousand of them all, do praise;
The *Day* which all Enlightned minds confess,
The Day-break of Eternal Blessedness;
The Day; Incomparable Day; so fair   175
None among all *Times* flying Children are:
The *Map of Heaven*, the *Light of Earth*, or which
God from Deep *Treasures* does our Souls Enrich.

She Lov'd the Day, She Lov'd the LORD, of whom
The *Day* proclaim'd his *Rising* from the *Tomb*.   180
MARY this Day knew what it was to have
Joy in a JESUS *Rising* from the Grave.
    Bright Day, Thou *Soul* of Piety; we see
    All True Religion Lives or Dyes with thee.
My *Heroine* saw this, and kept the Day;   185
This was, or None, She saw, to Heav'n the way.
Vain Things Lay by; but with a Zealous Heart,
Now MARY chose and sought the *Better part*.
So on THIS DAY at last She must Expire,
And to a *Sacred Rest* with CHRIST Retire.   190
The *Seventh* and the *Sacred Day*, the *Dove*
Takes for her Flight unto the *Ark* above.

    O Chrysostom, Revoke thy gross Abuse;
    How could a *Golden Mouth* such *Dross* produce?
    A WOMAN, as *True Friendships* Enemy,   195
    True Evil but Good painted, to decry?
    What *Mother* had the *Father* op'ning thus?
    Or was he but a *Terræ Filius*?[17]

An Admirable MARY does refute
The Clamour, and strike Ev'ry *Satyr* mute.   200
    But stay; Bold Quill; Touch not that String
                too Long
Lest *Length* may do at *Length* her Vertue wrong.
Who knew her need no Verse of mine; for they
Know more than my Imperfect Verse can say.   205
Who knew her not, will vainly think that none
Can say beyond that which by *me* was known.
My Pen so *Silenc'd* will by Silence speak
It self to Celebrate her Praise too weak.
Tell only What's her Fate, or, *That She's Dead;*   210
Twill be impossible then to proceed.

A BIRTH of *One*, to *Both* a Death becomes;
A Breathless Mother the *Dead Child* Entomb's.
Sad Fate! But for another BIRTH we wait:
She and her *Infant*, will be *Twins* in That.   215
With *Tears* that cannot stop, till then we must
Behold a *Diamond* Lying in the Dust.

A Lacrymatory:
Design'd for the *Tears* let fall at the Funeral of Mrs. SARAH LEVERET;[1] Who *Dy*'d 2d. 11 M. 1704,5.

Flow on, *Just Tears,* and let such *Dues* be paid:
Tears were at first, for these Occasions made.

    Long did I Vex in Vain at Stupid Man,
That e're Men found out Painting, so long Ages ran.
Fain would I *Painted* to the Life have seen   5
The *Heroines* that in past Times have been.
O could we Present that bright SARAH View,
Who *Mortals* charm'd, and who pleas'd *Angels* too.
Or that brave MIRIAM, She of whom tis said,
The *Israels* Daughters in Devotions *Led:*   10
Could *glorious* DEBORAH appear agen,
And to true *Glory* Quicken Slothful Men:
Could *Prayerful* Hannah once again be shown,
Prostrate in *Prayer's* before the Sapphire Throne:
Could *Pious* MARY with her inward worth,   15
And all her *Piety* again come forth:
We'd *Love* the *Painter,* and admire the skill;
But tis our *Grief,* we want that *Painting* Still.
And courteous *Dorcas,* we complain of Thee
We can't thy Face wrought with thy *Needle* see.   20
    But now there is an end of all complaints;
ONE Matron gives a sight of *all* the *Saints.*
Our LEV'RET is of all a curious Draught:
Oh! what an one! by what fine Pencil wrought
    So on one *Cherry-Stone,* true Fame avers,   25
    Vienna showes an Hundred Pourtraiters.

So *Hamborough*[2] does of an *Agate* tell,
Where *Europes* Princely Faces all do dwell.
The *Siamese* their Golden Image prize
Whose Price does to Twelve Million *Livres* rise.   30
VIRTUE a Nobler Image did Erect
In our Incomparable LEVERET.
   Vain Jews, The *Palaces* no more Divide
Where Holy Women do in *Heav'n* reside:
Four Præsidents assign to them no more;   35
Or say, a *Fifth's* now added to the Four.
   She shall be *Ours* on *Earth* at least; and we
By this our HULDAH[3] will directed be.
You, Ladies, that were *Tutoresses* to
The Ancient Sages, *did*, what she shall do.   40

   'O VIRGINS worthy of the *Zodiack*, Love
'Those Objects first and most, that are Above.
'Be first *Espous'd* unto the mighty LORD,
'On Terms propos'd in his most Sacred Word.
'Walk not with them whose *Folly* leads to Hell;   45
'By awful *Modesty* rude *Fools* repell.
'Let not *Vile Books* your blooming years deprave,
'But *Books* of *Grace* let your perusal have.
'Rather to *Churches* than to Balls repair;
'Perfume you *Closets* too with *Daily Prayer*.   50
'*Foul Cards* let your *Fair Hands* throw by with Scorn
'But *Write* and *Work* as for high purpose born.
'Let pearly *Tears* (at which lewd wretches scoff)
'Of *Penitence* wash your *Black Patches* off.
Dress well; *Flant* not too high; nor *Change* too fast.   55
Wear what shall speak you *Sober, Wise* and *Chast,*
And in a *Body* clad with comely Dress,
Soul drest with rich *Robes of Righteousness.*
Thus did our admirable SARAH: Thus
Of *Virgin-Grace* a mould she left for us.   60
Her *Matchless Merits* now prepared her
To be a *Match* for a great GOVERNOUR.
Him *Sarah* call'd Her *Lord:* Himself to please
She sought: And saw none but her *Tygranes.*
The *Colony* in her sweet carriage saw   65
What made in *every House* a *Persian* Law.
A *Wife* so lovely, so discreet and kind;
How Bles'd of God, the Man that shall her find!

81

Rise up, Her Daughters, and with *Grace* Repeat,
How she did You with constant *Wisdom* treat.   70
Do what she *did* for You; And still Retain
What she gave You of *Tincture in the Grain.*
O Happy *Chickens*! [Those we *Happy* sing;]
Whom such a Dam warms with her Tender Wing.
She must a *Widow* too Example give   75
How in a Patient *Widow-Hood* to live.
Dead her *Patricius* Twenty years and five,
Deathless did in his moaning *Dove* Survive.
Her *Maker* now she did her *Husband* make:
Such Souls in *Him* can full contentment take.   80
With Famous Women let our SARAH claim
For best endowments an Immortal Name.
Hippatia[4] taught of old the *Liberal Arts*:
But *Ours* the Art of managing our Hearts.
Eudoxia[5] *Glosses* on the Bible wrote;   85
But *Ours* a *Gloss* in her pure practice brought.
Rosuida[6] wrote the *Lives* of worthy Men:
Ours liv'd one *Worthy to be wrote* by them.
With *Zealous Visits* to the *House of* God,
A mansion there she chose for her Abode.   90
Her *Fervent Zeal* would overcome the *Cold*:
No *Storms* from Coming there could her withold.
   Ye, Men of God, Your *Funeral-Sermons* owe
   For Her who *Sermons* those Regards did show.
   You have in Her an Auditory gone,   95
   A Full one t'was, if she were there Alone.
Good Lady, Tell us now that *Secret Rare;*
Rare like the *Stone* of the *Philosopher:*
A Life of *Ten Times Seven Years* to run.
And *all that while to be Reproach'd by None.*   100
   None You *Reproach'd,* But every Person knew
   What *Good* You could, You'd every Person do
   There *Madam,* lay Your Skill: By *Goodness* tis
   We charm fell *Serpents,* that they cannot hiss.
Till grown for *Earth* too Good, on *Earth* she grew   105
Heav'n claim'd her then: and then to *Heav'n* she flew.
   Luxurious Death; such *Pearls* to Swallow thus!
   Fam'd *Cleopatra's* Draught was less profuse.
You rash *Astronomers,* the Stars miscall,
A *Dog* you style the brightest of them all.   110
Correct an Error which You find so *Great;*

82

Your *Sirius*[7] now shall be a LEVERET.
Else the most Fulgid *Lamp,* which Heav'n did show
And then took in an Hundred Years ago,
Now She's got there, will once again appear,   115
And radiant Sit in *Cassiopea's* Chair.[8]

    Lacrymatories, which Reserv'd of old
Tears for the *Dead,* were *Viols* (as we're told:)
Our LEVERET is *Lost;* we'l *Weep* for her
Tears that shall fill the Tun of *Heidelbergh.*[9]   120

On the GRAVES,
OF MY
Young Brethren,[1]
[*Carent quia vate Sacro.*][2]

Graves! Where in Dust are laid our dearest *Hopes!*
Pay, *Passengers,* your *Tributary Drops.*
Your *Tears* Allow'd, yea, *Hallowed* now become,
Since *Tears* were drop't by JESUS on a *Tomb.*
Churches, Weep on; & Wounded yield your *Tears;*   5
Tears use to flow from hack't *New-English Firrs.*
    Zion, Thy *Sons* are gone; Tho' men might see
This and that Man, brave Men, were *born in thee.*
Tell, what they were; Let thy *True Trumpet* tell
Truth of the *Sons of Truth,* and how they fell.   10
Sure, when our *Sev'n* did to their Seats retire,
Th' Harmonious *Nine* did not with them expire.
Smooth Numbers first were form'd for Themes like these;
T' immortalize deserving *Memories.*

    First, *What they were not,* Say; for they were *Not*   15
Such as their *Mother* might account a Blot.
    Not such as to the *Sacred Priest-hood* fly,
Meerly as to a *Craft,* to Live thereby.
Not, who at *Church* seem *Serious* and *Demure,*
But out of it, no *Strictness* can Endure.   20
Not those who dare *Jest* with Gods awful Word
And Lewdly can *Play* with the *Flaming Sword.*

Not the *Black* Folks, where nothing *White* we know
But what an *Open'd Mouth* may chance to show.
Not *Snuffs*, instead of *Stars*; (the Room, no doubt,   25
Would Sweeter be, if *Such* were turned out.)
Not *Blind-men*, [So the *Talmuds* reckon them!]
Who *Dark* themselves, hold *Lights* to other men.
Not *Lads*, whom for their *Levity* alone
The Punning Tribe, *De Tribu Levi*, own.   30
Not who to *Pulpits* hop Unfledg'd, and there
Talk twice a *Week*, and *Preach* not once a year.
Not those who do the *Pious Neighbour* Shun,
But to the Wicked *Sons of Belial* run.
Not those who hate their Work, as Boyes the *Rod*,   35
And hate and flout *Laborious* Men of *God*.
     If such there are; *Take, Lord, thy Holy Scourge,*
     And from such Nusances, thy Temple Purge!

Not such my Sons; by *Zion* so we're told;
Sons comparable to the Finest Gold.   40
     But, *What they were*, Fair Lady, canst thou say,
What thy Lost *Seven*, and not faint away!
     For with her *Seven Sons*, and such as these,
     Dy'd the brave Mother of the *Maccabees*.[3]
Mirrours of Piety they were, and knew   45
Betimes, how to be Wise and Good and True.
Early the *Larks* Praise to their Maker Sung;
So Saint *Macarius*, *Old* while very *Young*.
The Towns to which they did their Toyls dispense,
Them their Bright *Glory* thought, & Strong *Defence*.   50
The *Tears* of their Bereaved Flocks Proclame
More than could Marble *Pyramids* their Name.
These were *N. Englands Pride*; But Humbly Show'd
Men might be *so*, and not *themselves* be *Proud*.
Dryden Sayes, *Look the Reformation round*,   55
No Treatise of Humility *is found*.
Dryden, Thou Ly'st; They *Write*, and more than so.
They *Live Humility*; they can be *low*.
Low these were always in their own *Esteem*,
But the more *highly* we Esteemed them.   60
Low-roof'd the *Temples*, but more Stately than
St. *Sophy's*, built by Great *Justinian*,[4]
The *Proud* might trample on them as on *Earth*,

84

But glorious *Mines of Worth* lay underneath.
    First they did all to *Kiriath-Sepher*⁵ go;   65
And *then* a *Church* did Heav'n on them bestow.
By Learning first their *Lamps* were made to Blaze;
And *Incense* each *then* on the *Altar* layes.
The *Liberal Arts* they knew; but understood
Most Thine, Great *Antonine;*⁶ That, [*To be Good.*]   70
And *Good to Do,* This was their main Delight;
For *This* they did all *Youths* vain Pleasure Sleight.
    While such rare Youths must Dy, no *Lawyers* wit
    (Not *Asgils*)⁷ can *abate Death's Fatal Writ.*
    Must such see but a *Finger* of the *Span*   75
    That is to measure the Frail *Life* of man!
    Yet we'l demand *Eternity* for them;
    And they shall Live too in *Eternal Fame.*
Reckon, O Jews, your *Priestly Blemishes,*
Forty above an *Hundred,* if you please: 80
A *Priest* for each of these did lose his call;
But *Ours* to all appear'd still free from all.
The Power of your fine *Loadstones,* wondrous Great,
Report, *ye Masters of the Cabinet:*
Loadstones in weight a *Dram*; well-Shodden they   85
Pull up what near *Two Hundred Drams* will weigh.
Our *Potent Loadstones* more attractive were;
And more the *Sphere of their Activity* extended far.
    Now, *Pancirol,*⁸ upon my honest Word,
The Lost *Sepulchral Lamps,* are Now Restor'd.   90
Our *Saints,* to whom do Serve as *Oyl,* our *Tears,*
Bright *Lamps,* they glare still in their *Sepulchres.*

    My CLARK was One. And such a *Clark* as he
Synods of *Angels* would take *Theirs* to be.
Faintly to Praise a Youth of such Desert,   95
Were but to Shoot indeed vile *Slanders* Dart.
See but his *Wasted Flesh*; T'was Flaming *Zeal*
That Melted him: The Flame is burning still.
Methinks I see his Ravish'd Hearers wait
And long to hear still his next *Heav'nly Treat.*   100
Look; The Fat Cloud, what *Oracles* he pours
On Thirsty Souls in most *Expedient Showres!*
His *Preaching* much, but more his *Practice* wrought
A *Living Sermon* of the Truths he *Taught.*

So all might *See* the *Doctrines* which they *Heard*,   105
And way to *Application* fairly clear'd.
Strong were the *Charms* of that Sinceritie
Which made his *Works* well with his *Words* agree.
    Painter, Thy Pencils take. Draw first, a *Face*
Shining, (but by himself not seen) with *Grace*.   110
An Heav'n touch'd *Eye*, where [what of *Kens* is told]
One might, MY GOD, in *Capitals* behold.
A *Mouth*, from whence a *Label* shall proceed,
And [O LOVE CHRIST] the *Motto* to be Read.
An *Hand* still open to relieve the Poor,   115
And by *Dispersing* to *increase* the Store.
    Such was my CLARK; so did he *Look*, and so
Much more than *Look*, or *Speak*, so did he *Do*.
Botanists, Boast your *Palm-Tree*, whence arise
More than Three Hundred rich Commodities.   120
Write, *Persian Poet*, that brave Tree to Praise,
As many *Songs* as in the year be *Dayes*.
My CLARK more *Vertues* had; So must the Tree
Too rich for *Earth*, to *Heav'n* transplanted be.
HUBBARD Another. When the Youth they saw,   125
So *Wise*, Their *Love* he challeng'd, & their *Awe*.
Older Spectators fed their wondring Eyes,
With *Love*, to see Young Children grow so *Wise*.
Envy her self grew weary of her *Gall*,
And gave Consent, he should be *Lov'd* by all.   130
The *Pastoral* of *Gregory* the Great,
Won't Say how well he fill'd the *Pastors* Seat.
In Saving Souls his Happy Hours he spent,
And Preach'd *Salvation* wheresoe're he went.
A *Cassius*,⁹ whom the Hearers did attend,   135
With constant *Fear*, that he would make an *End*.
His *Life* a *Letter*, where the World might Spell
Great *Basils* Morals,¹⁰ and his Death the *Seal*.
The *Graces* which were *Sparks* on *Earth* below,
To Glorious *Flames* in *Heav'n* they now do grow.   140
Oh! Should a *Star* drop from the Sky to us,
We should with Reverence admire it thus!
For such a Child of *Jacob* there Unite
Th' *Egyptian* Weeping with the *Israelite*.
So has his *After-Beams* the Setting *Sun*;   145
Tho' he be *Set*, his Splendor is not gone.

Adieu, My CLARK, my HUBBARD, thus Adieu;
A *Pair* well *Parallel'd* we had in you.
Grave *Plutarch*,[11] Hadst thou Liv'd till now, the *Pair*
Would have Engross'd thy Pen, they Look so fair.　　150
Such Gifts as these, by Heav'n bestow'd on Men,
Must just be *Show'n*, and then call'd back agen!
Lord, Why so soon, such *Fruitful Trees* cut down!
No *Wood* of Such, was on the *Altar* known.
Trees not cut down, [the Glorious Answer is,]　　155
But all Translated into Paradise.
From the *Quick Seizure* of the greedy *Grave*
Her Darling *Sons* my Country cannot Save.
But, *Grave*, Thou shalt not so thy Prey consume,
As ever *Buried in Oblivions* Womb.　　160
Thus *Thetis*[12] Comforted her *Short-Liv'd* Son,
Dy Young, Long shalt thou be Admir'd when Dead & Gone.
　　One of the *Pleiades* long since withdrew.[13]
　　And Heav'n but *Six*, does of the *Seven* shew.
　　If all the rest should chance to hide their Face,　　165
　　My *Seven Stars* may well Supply their Place.
Now, hold, my Pen; *Plato* of old would have
But *Four Heroick Lines* upon a Grave.

Help me, my God, at Work like them to be;
And take their Deaths as Watch-words unto me.　　170

Ex *Paulini* Panegyrico in Obitum Celsi.

Heu, quid agam? Dubia Pendens Pietate Laboro,
　　Gratuler an Doleam? Dignus utroque Puer.
Cujus Amor Lacrymas et Amor mihi Gaudia Suadet;
　　Sed Gaudere Fides, Flere jubet Pietas.
Tam Modicum Patribus, tam dulci e pigmore Fructum
　　Defleo in Exiguo Temporis esse datum.
Lætor Obisse brevi functum Mortalia Seclo,
　　Ut cito divinas Consequeretur Opes.[14]

GRATITUDINIS ERGO,
An ESSAY on the Memory of my
Venerable MASTER;
Ezekiel Cheever.[1]

Augusto perstringere Carmine Laudes,
Quas nulla Eloquij vis Celebrare queat.[2]

You that are *Men* & Thoughts of *Manhood* know,
Be Just now to the *Man* that made you so.
Martyred by *Scholars* the stabb'd *Cassian*[3] dies.
And falls to cursed Lads a Sacrifice.
Not so my CHEEVER; Not by *Scholars* slain,   5
But Prais'd, and Lov'd, and wish'd to *Life* again.
Almighty *Tribe* of Well-instructed Youth
Tell what they owe to him, and Tell with Truth.
All the *Eight parts of Speech* he taught to them
They now Employ to *Trumpet* his Esteem.   10
They fill *Fames Trumpet,* and they spread a Fame
To last till the *Last Trumpet* drown the same.
Magister[4] pleas'd them well, because 'twas *he*;
They saw that *Bonus*[5] did with it agree.
While they said, *Amo,*[6] they the Hint improve   15
Him for to make the Object of their *Love.*
No *Concord* so Inviolate they knew
As to pay Honours to their Master due.
With *Interjections* they break off at last,
But, *Ah,* is all they use, *Wo,* and, *Alas!*   20
We Learnt *Prosodia,* but with that Design
Our Masters Name should in our *Verses* shine.
Our Weeping *Ovid* but instructed us
To write upon *his* Death, *De Tristibus.*[7]
Tully[8] we read, but still with this Intent,   25
That in *his* praise we might be Eloquent.
Our Stately *Virgil* made us but Contrive
As our *Anchises* to keep *him* Alive,
When *Phænix* to *Achilles* was assign'd
A *Master,* then we thought not *Homer* blind.   30
A *Phænix,* which Oh! might his *Ashes* shew!
So rare a Thing we thought *our Master* too.
And if we made a *Theme,* 'twas with Regret

88

We might not on *his* Worth show all our Wit.
   Go on, ye Grateful Scholars, to proclame 35
To late Posterity your *Masters* Name.
Let it as many Languages declare
As on *Loretto*-Table do appear.
   Too much to be by any *one* exprest:
   I'll tell my share, and *you* shall tell the rest. 40
Ink is too vile a Liquor; *Liquid Gold*
Should fill the Pen, by which such things are told.
The book should Amyanthus-Paper be
All writ with *Gold*, from all corruption free.
   A Learned Master of the *Languages* 45
Which to Rich *Stores* of Learning are the *Keyes;*
He taught us first *Good Sense* to understand
And put the *Golden Keyes* into our Hand,
We but for him had been for Learning *Dumb,*
And had a sort of *Turkish Mutes* become. 50
Were *Grammar* quite Extinct, yet at his Brain
The *Candle* might have well been lit again.
If *Rhet'rick* had been stript of all her *Pride*
She from his *Wardrobe* might have been Supply'd.
Do but Name CHEEVER, and the *Echo* straight 55
Upon that Name, *Good Latin,* will Repeat.
A *Christian Terence,*[9] Master of the *File*
That arms the Curious to Reform their *Style.*
Now *Rome* and *Athens* from their Ashes rise;
See their *Platonick Year* with vast surprise: 60
And in our *School* a *Miracle* is Wrought;
For the *Dead Languages* to *Life* are brought.
   His *Work* he Lov'd: Oh! had we done the same:
Our *Play-dayes* still to him ungrateful came.
And yet so well our *Work* adjusted Lay, 65
We came to *Work,* as if we came to *Play.*
   Our *Lads* had been, but for his wondrous Cares,
   Boyes of my Lady *Mores*[10] unquiet Pray'rs.
   Sure were it not for such informing *Schools,*
   Our *Lat'ran* too would soon be fill'd with *Owles.* 70
Tis CORLET's[11] pains, & CHEEVER's, we must own,
That thou, *New-England,* art not *Scythia* grown.
The *Isles* of *Silly*[12] had o're-run this Day
The *Continent* of our *America.*
Grammar he taught, which 'twas his work to do: 75
But he would *Hagar*[13] have her place to know.

89

The *Bible* is the Sacred *Grammar,* where
The *Rules of speaking well,* contained are.
He taught us *Lilly,*[14] and he *Gospel* taught;
And us poor Children to our *Saviour* brought.   80
Master of Sentences, he gave us more
Then we in our *Sententia* had before.
We Learn't Good Things in *Tullies Offices;*
But we from *him* Learn't Better things than these.
With *Cato's*[15] he to us the *Higher* gave   85
Lessons of JESUS, that our Souls do save.
We Constru'd *Ovid's Metamorphosis,*
But on our selves charg'd, not a *Change* to miss.
Young *Austin*[16] wept, when he saw *Dido*[17] dead,
Tho' not a Tear for a *Lost Soul* he had: 90
Our Master would not let us be so vain,
But us from *Virgil* did to *David* train,
Textors Epistles would not *Cloathe* our Souls;
Pauls too we heard; we *went to School at Pauls.*

Syrs, Do you not Remember well the Times,   95
When us he warn'd against our *Youthful Crimes:*
What *Honey dropt* from our old *Nestors*[18] mouth
When with his Counsels he Reform'd our Youth:
How much he did to make us *Wise* and *Good;*
And with what *Prayers,* his work he did conclude.   100
Concern'd, that when from him we *Learning* had,
It might not *Armed Wickedness* be made!
The *Sun* shall first the *Zodiac* forsake,
And *Stones* unto the *Stars* their Flight shall make:
First shall the *Summer* bring large drifts of *Snow,*   105
And beauteous Cherries in *December* grow;
E're of those Charges we Forgetful are
Which we, *O man of God,* from thee did hear.
　　Such *Tutors* to the *Little Ones* would be
　　Such that *in Flesh* we should *their Angels* see,   110
　　Ezekiel should not be the Name of such;
　　We'd *Agathangelus*[19] not think too much,
Who Serv'd the *School,* the *Church* did not forget,
But Thought, and Pray'd, and often wept for it.
Mighty in Prayer: How did he wield thee, Pray'r!   115
Thou Reverst Thunder: CHRIST's-Sides-piercing Spear?
Soaring we saw the *Birds of Paradise;*
So Wing'd by Thee, for Flights beyond the Skies.
How oft we saw him tread the *Milky Way,*

Which to the Glorious *Throne of Mercy* lay!   120
 Come from the *Mount,* he shone with ancient Grace.
Awful the *Splendor* of his Aged Face
Cloath'd in the *Good Old Way,* his Garb did wage
A War with the Vain Fashions of the Age.
Fearful of nothing more than hateful *Sin;*   125
'Twas that from which he laboured all to win,
Zealous; And in *Truths Cause* ne'r known to trim;
No *Neuter Gender* there allow'd by him.
Stars but a *Thousand* did the Ancients know;
On later Globes they *Nineteen hundred* grow: 130
Now such a CHEEVER added to the Sphere;
Makes an Addition to the *Lustre* there.
 Mean time *America* a *Wonder* saw;
A Youth in Age, forbid by *Natures* Law.
 You that in t'other Hemisphere do dwell,   135
Do of *Old Age* your dismal Stories tell.
You tell of *Snowy Heads* and *Rheumy Eyes*
And things that make a man himself despise.
You say, a *frozen Liquor* chills the Veins,
And scarce the *Shadow* of a *Man* remains.   140
Winter of Life, that *sapless Age* you call,
And of all Maladies the *Hospital*
The *Second Nonage* of the Soul; the *Brain*
Cover'd with Cloud; the *Body* all in pain.
To weak *Old Age,* you say, there must belong   145
A Trembling Palsey both of *Limb* and *Tongue;*
Dayes all Decrepit, and a Bending *Back,*
Propt by a *Staff,* in *Hands* that ever Shake.
 Nay, Syrs, our CHEEVER shall confute you all,
On whom there did none of these Mischefs fall.   150
He *Liv'd,* and to vast Age no Illness knew;
'Till *Time's Scythe* waiting for him Rusty grew.
He *Liv'd* and *Wrought,* His Labour's were Immense;
But ne'er *Declin'd* to Præter-perfect Tense.
A *Blooming Youth* in him at *Ninety Four*   155
We saw; But, Oh! when such a sight before!
At Wondrous *Age* he did his *Youth* resume,
As when the *Eagle* mew's his Aged plume.
With Faculties of *Reason* still so bright
And at Good Services so Exquisite   160
Sure our sound Chiliast, we wondring thought,
To the *First Ressurection* is not brought!

No, He for That was waiting at the Gate
In the *Pure Things* that fit a Candidate.
He in Good Actions did his Life Employ,   165
And to make others Good, he made his Joy.
Thus well-appris'd now of the *Life to Come,*
To *Live here* was to him a *Martyrdom:*
Our brave *Macrobius*[20] Long'd to see the Day
Which others dread, of being *Call'd away.*   170
So, Ripe with Age, he does invite the Hook
Which watchful does for its large Harvest look.
Death gently cut the *Stalk,* and kindly laid
Him, where our God His *Granary* has made.
    Who at *New-Haven* first began to Teach,   175
Dying *Unshipwreck'd,* does *White-Haven* reach.
At that *Fair Haven* they all Storms forget;
He there his DAVENPORT[21] with Love does meet.
    The *Luminous Robe,* the *Loss* whereof with *Shame*
Our Parents wept, when *Naked* they became;   180
Those Lovely *Spirits* wear it, and therein
Serve God with *Priestly Glory,* free from Sin.
    But in his *Paradisian Rest* above,
To *Us* does the Blest Shade retain his Love.
With *Rip'ned Thoughts* Above concern'd for Us,   185
We can't but hear him dart his Wishes, thus.
    'TUTORS, Be *Strict;* But yet be *Gentle* too:
'Don't by fierce *Cruelties* fair *Hopes* undo.
'Dream not, that they who are to Learning slow,
'Will mend by Arguments in *Ferro.*[22]   190
'Who keeps the *Golden Fleece,* Oh, let him not
'A *Dragon* be, tho' he *Three Tongues* have got.
'Why can you not to Learning find the way,
'But thro' the Province of *Severia?*
'Twas *Moderatus,* who taught *Origen;*[23]   195
'A *Youth* which prov'd one of the Best of men.
'The Lads with *Honour* first, and *Reason* Rule;
'*Blowes* are but for the *Refractory Fool.*
'But, Oh! First Teach them their Great God to fear;
'That you like me, with joy may meet them here.   200
               He has said!
Adieu, a little while, Dear Saint, Adieu;
Your *Scholar* won't be Long, Sir, after you.
In the mean time, with Gratitude I must
Engrave an EPITAPH upon your Dust.   205

'Tis true, *Excessive Merits* rarely safe:
Such an *Excess* forfeits an *Epitaph*.
But if Base men the Rules of Justice break,
The *Stones* (at least upon the *Tombs*) will speak.

Et Tumulum facite, et Tumulo superaddite carmen.[24]
(Virg. in Daphn.)

EPITAPHIUM.
EZEKIEL CHEEVERUS.

Ludimagister:
Primo Neo-portensis;
Deinde, Ipsuicensis;
Postea, Carolotenensis
Postremo, Bostonensis
cujus
Doctrinam ac Virtutem
Nosti, si Sis Nov-Anglus,
Colis, si non Barbarus;
GRAMMATICUS,
a Quo, non pure tantum, sed et pie,
Loqui;
RHETORICUS,
a Quo non tantum Ornate dicere
coram Hominibus,
Sed et Orationes coram Deo fundere
Efficacissimas;
POETA,
a Quo non tantum Carmina pangere,
Sed et
Cælestes Hymnos, Odasq; Angelicas,
canere,
Didicerunt,
Qui discere voluerunt;
LUCERNA,
ad Quam accensa sunt,
Quis queat numerare,
Quot Ecclesiarum Lumina?
ET

93

Qui secum Corpus Theologiæ abstulit,
Peritissimus THEOLOGUS,
Corpus hic suum sibi minus Charum,
deposuit.
Vixit Annos, XCIV.
Docuit, Annos, LXX.
Obijt, A.D. M. DCC. VIII.
Et quod Mori potuit,
HEIC
Expectet Exoptatq:
Primam Sanctorum Ressurectionem
ad
Immortalitatem.
Evuvijs debetur Honos Immortalitatem primam.[25]

EPITAPH

DUMMER,[1] the *Shephard* Sacrific'd
By *Wolves,* because the *Sheep* he Priz'd;
The *Orphans* Father, Churches Light,
The *Love* of Heaven, of Hell the *Spite;*
The Countreyes *Gapman,* and the *Face*   5
That *Shone,* but *Knew* it not, with Grace.

DUMMER, a *Wise man* of the *East,*
Gone to see JESUS, in His *Rest:*
Hunted by *Divels,* but Reliev'd
By *Angels,* and on High Reciev'd: 10

The Martyr'd *Pelican,* who *Bled,*
Rather than Leave the Saints *Unfed,*

DUMMER, the *Bird of Paradise,*
Shot, and *Flown* thither in a trice;
Methus'la Dead, from whence our *Flood,*   15
Threefold of *Tears & Fears & Blood;*
HERE Left his *Ashes,* and we see,
Gods *Temple* thus in *Ashes!*————

LORD, Hear the *Cry of Righteous* DUMMERS Wounds,
Under thine *Altar;* Lord, Rate off those *Hounds*   20

That Worry thus thy *Flocks:* And let the *Bones*
Of thine ELISHA,[2] over whom our Moans
Are Sigh'd, Inspire the *Life* of *Zeal* into
The Rest, that have a *Work,* Like *His* to Do.

The Excellent WIGGLESWORTH,[1]
Remembred by some Good Tokens.

HIS Pen did once Meat from the Eater fetch;
And now he's gone beyond the *Eaters* reach.
His *Body,* once so *Thin,* was next to *None;*
From Thence, he's to *Unbodied Spirits flown.*
Once his rare skill did all *Diseases* heal;   5
And he does nothing now *uneasy* feel.
He to his *Paradise* is Joyful come;
And waits with Joy to see his Day of Doom.

95

Part Three: Verse for Children

Some *SCRIPTURAL* HYMNS
FOR
Children.

[I.] Little Children
Brought unto the Lord JESUS CHRIST.

On *Mat.* XIX. 14.
When *Little Children* once were brought
 To our most Gracious Lord:
Them that Oppos'd, He better Taught,
 By this most precious Word:

'*Suffer* Your *Little Children,* so,   5
 '*Forbid* them not, I say,
'*Their* Saviour to *come* unto;
 'I'm *He,* and *come* they may.

'Acknowledge me a mighty *King,*
 'That *Heavenly Graces* give;   10
'*Infants* to me, for *Subjects* bring;
 '*My Heaven* does *them* receive.

Thus does our Blessed *Shepherd* call,
 Our *lambs* into His *Fold:*
Lord pour thy *Blessings* on them all,   15
 Blessings richer than Gold.

Oh! What a Glorious *Grace* is This,
 Which God through Christ will grant,
That HE *ours* and *our Childrens* is,
 In His Best *Covenant.*   20

99

[II.] Early Religion.

1 *King.* XVIII.
O That while I am *Young* I might
   Fear the most Glorious One;
And not my Great *Redeemer* Slight:
   Thine, Lord; I'm THINE alone.

2 *Chron.* 34–3.
May I while I am very *Young,*
   Seek unto God by *Prayer:*
And those *Lov'd* Ones be found among
   That *Early Seekers* are:

Psal. 119.9.
May I, while I am *Young,* give Heed
   Unto thy *Holy* Word;
Call'd, there to *Cleanse* my wayes with Speed,
   By the most *Holy Lord.*

2 *Joh.* 4.
Though I am yet a *Child,* I wou'd
   In my most Forward *Youth,*
Walk, by the conduct of my God,
   In the *pure* paths of *Truth.*

2 *Tim.* 2.22.
Those *Lusts* that *Youthful* are, to me
   May they most *Hateful* prove;
And may the *Laws* of JESUS be
   My Sweetest Joy and Love.

Eccl. 12.1.
Lord, *THEE,* my Maker, Thee, To Day,
   God, *Father, Son,* and *Spirit,*
I would *Remember,* that I may
   Eternal Life Inherit.

[III.] The Consent of the Believer
unto the Ten Commandments.

LORD, I should have no *Lord*, beside
Thee, to be Lov'd, Serv'd, *Glorify'd*.
I should the *Glory* due to Thee,
In *Wayes*, pay, that *Appointed* be.

Thy *Names*, Thy *Words*, Thy *Works*, I should,   5
Sacred for *proper Uses*, hold.
The *Dayes* which thou made *Sacred* hath,
I should not in *Diversions* wast.

In their Fit *places*, every one,
I should with all *Fit Honours* own.   10
That *Life* none may unjustly Loose,
Means I should with all kindness use.

Chast I should be in every *part*,
Yea, *Chast* in every *Thought* of Heart.
To *Get* and *Keep* my Worldly *Wealth*,   15
I should commit no sort of *Stealth*.

Truth I should utter, and *maintain*,
And no *Good Name* with *Slander* stain.
With sweet *Content* I should Receive
All the *Wise God* will please to give.   20

Lord, By the *Blood of* CHRIST, I pray,
Save me, who do not thus obey;
And by the *Strength* of CHRIST, from hence,
Sav'd, Let me yield Obedience.

[IV.] The Lords Prayer.

Our Father, in the Heavenly Throne,
Inclin'd from thence to Help us all;
For the Sake of thy Blessed *Son*,
Thy *Children* thus upon Thee Call.

We would thy Ever-glorious *Name,*   5
As *Holy,* with Great Fear Adore:
And wish that All may in the same,
Thy *Holy One Praise* Evermore.

May thy Just *Kingdom Come,* we Pray
That thou art *the Worlds King,* we know: 10
But, Oh! bring on that Happy Day,
When all *the World* shall own Thee so.

May we thy Righteous *Will* approve,
And it all Things commanding see,
As it in the *New Heaven* above,   15
And the *New Earth* below, shall be.

Lord, Give us a *Convenient Food;*
What may be *Such,* to *Thee* we leave,
And let us not want *any Good;*
All we Rely on *Thee* to give.   20

Our *Faults,* by which we are in *Debt*
To Thy dread Justice, Lord, Release:
Christ Payes our *Debt;* And we Forget,
For *this,* our Neighbours Injuries.

We're Frail; Us from *Temptation* Save;   25
Sins, Oh! *Sins,* The *worst Evils* are:
Us Let not *Evil Tempters* have,
And hold in any Sinful *Snare.*

Thou hast the *Rule* of All; A Word
Of thine can *Do* All: To Thee then   30
All *Honour's* due: We Shout, O Lord,
AMEN, in *Faith* of thy, AMEN!

[V.] The Lords-Day.

On *Rev.* I. 10.
This is the *Day of Rest,* whereon
Our Lord *Rose* from the Dead;
The Price of mans *Redemption,*
This Day was fully paid.

This is to us, the *Joyful* Day,   5
   Which our *Lord* made His *own*,
By his most *Wonderful* Display
   Of *Pow'r* and *Grace* thereon.

The *Jewish Sabbath* Laid *Asleep*
   With our *Lord* under Earth,   10
Directs us Now *This Day* to keep
   Of our Lords *Second Birth*.

This is the *Day,* our *Lord* now chose
   Thereon still to *Appear;*
The *Day,* for Him *preferr'd* by Those   15
   That His *Apostles* were.

It is Declar'd, *The Lords-Day,* Now,
   Holy unto the *Lord*
It will no *Worldly Thought* allow,
   No Worldly *Work* or *Word*.   20

Now, *Lord,* on this *Thy Day,* dispence,
   Thy *Spirit* unto me:
And by thy *Spirits* Influence
   Let me now *Acted* be.

This Day, Oh! *Spirit,* from on High,   25
   Make thou a *Mean* and *Sign,*
Of that *Great Sabbacism,* when I
   Shall in thy *Glory* shine!

[VI.] Prayer Encouraged.

Matth. 7.7–11. with *Luk.* II.9.13.

That Lord, on whose Account alone
   Our *Pray'rs* prevail with God,
Bids us Address that Glorious One,
   With *Prayers* for Ev'ry Good.

Ask now, and ye shall *have,* (saith He)   5
   'Seek now, and ye shall *find*.

'Heav'ns Doors, at which you *Knocking* be,
  'Shall *Open* to your Mind.

'What *Father*, to a *Sons* Request
  'For *Bread* or *Fish*, will throw   10
'A *Stone* or *Snake?* His very best
  'He'l on a *Son* bestow.

'*God* is your *Better Father*; You
  'In me, *His Children* are;
You'l Gain, with His *Good Spirit* now,   15
  'All *Good Things* else, by Pray'r.

Joh. 16.23.

'*Children*, Then to the *Father* Go;
  'Go, in my Name, I say:
'Rich *Blessings*, He will give unto
  'Them, in that Name, who *Pray*.   20

Instructions for CHILDREN.

I. The Ancient *Creed*.

IN GOD the FATHER I Believe;
  He's the Almighty One.
I JESUS CHRIST, our *Lord, Receive,*
  God's Dear and Only SON.
I do Adore the Holy SPIRIT;   5
  Who is to *Raise the Dead,*
And bring His People to Inherit,
  Life that shall *never Fade*.

II. The Child's Resolution.

Help me *my God*! For unto thee
  I do Resolve to *Pray,*
To Grant thy *Christ* and *Grace* to me;
  I'll do it *every Day*.

Heavenly Father, *Give me thy* Christ;   5
Give me thy Spirit; *Pardon my Sins;*
Make me thy Servant; Bring me to thy
Kingdom; O Great GOD, who art Father,
and Son, and Holy Spirit; I Desire to be
Thine for evermore. Amen.   10

III. The Child at his *Food*.

At *Eating,* thus I ever shou'd
   Devout and *Thankful* be;
My God, I Bless thee for my Food;
   Let it be Bless'd to me.
A Child, that when he goes to *Eat,*   5
   Thinks not of GOD at all,
Is like the *Bruits,* which at their *Meat*
   On God do never call.

IV. The Child thinking on his *Baptism*.

Baptis'd for thee, O Glorious One,
   Thee for my GOD I take:
Thee will I *Love* and *Serve* alone;
   And *Thee* my *Portion* make.
My *Baptism* gave me unto thee;   5
   Possess me then, O Lord;
My *Father, Saviour, Leader* be,
   According to thy Word.

V. The Child on the Lord's Day.

My Saviour's *Risen* from the Dead,
   And Lives Enthron'd Above;
The *Price* of my *Salvation's* Paid,
   My *Life* is in His *Love.*
With *Holy Sabbaths* He, in *Peace,*   5
   Hath me *Victorious* blest;
Lord, Bring thou me, thro' *Holiness,*
   To *Victory,* and *Rest.*

VI. The Child seeing the Funeral of another Child.

I in the *Burying Place* may see
   Graves not so long as I.
From *Deaths Arrest* no Age is free;
   Young Children too may Dy.
My God, may such an awful sight   5
   Awakening be to me!
Oh! that by *Early Grace* I might
   For *Death* prepared be.

VII. The Body of Divinity Versifyed.

A GOD there is, a GOD of
      boundless Might,
In Wisdom, Justice, Goodness Infinite.
   [*Heb. XI.*6. *Psal. CXLVII.*5. *CXLV.*9,17.]
2. God is but *ONE*, & yet in *Persons Three*   5
The *Father, Son, & Spirit*, One God we see.
   [1 *Job. V.* 7.]
3. Our God, by His Great Name
      JEHOVAH Known
HE the *World Made*, and *Keeps*, and   10
      Rules Alone.
   [*Neh. IX.*6.]
4. To *Glorify* the Glorious GOD, is That
For which He did all Men, & me Create.
   [*Isai. XLI.* 21.]   15
5. God a Just *Rule* doth in our *Bible* give,
A *Rule*, both what to *Think*, and how
      to *Live*.
   [2 *Tim. III.* 15,16,17]
6. *Holy & Happy* our *First Parents* came   20
From Gods Hand, with *Gods Image* in
      our Frame.
   [*Gen. I.* 27.]
7. Tasting *Forbidden Fruit* our Parents *fell;*
This *Taste* has plung'd Mankind all   25
      down to *Hell.*
   [*Rom. V.* 12]
8. Our *Blest Lord* JESUS CHRIST,
      in our Distress,

Comes to fetch us from *Hell* to *Blessedness*.   30
        [*Luk. XIX*.10.]
9. Into His *Person*, the Bright *Son of God*
A *Virgins Son* took; There he makes
        Abode.
        [*Isa. VII.* 14.]   35
10. *Life* as a *Priest* CHRIST will His
        People bring,
Light as a *Prophet*, and *Law* as a *King*.
[Psal. *CX*.4. *Acts III*.22. *Isa. XXXIII*.22.]
11. For us our *Surety Liv'd*, for us He *Dy'd*,   40
And *Rising* did to *Heav'n* in *Triumph* Ride.
        [*Phil.* II. 7, 8, 9.]
12. By *Faith* to CHRIST we for
        Salvation go;
Faith too, as well as *That* must *He* bestow.   45
        [*Eph. II*.8.]
13. For *Sin* will the renew'd Believer
        Mourn,
And from all *Sin*, hee'l by *Repentance*
        Turn.   50
        [*Acts XX*.21.]
14. *Sinners* receiving of *Gods Pardon*, they
Gods Precept will, made *Saints*, with
        Love Obey.
        [*Tit. II.* 12,13,14.]   55
15. All *Homage* we must yield unto the
        Lord;
In all Directed, by his *Heavenly Word*.
His Works and *Names*, we may not use
        in Vain;   60
Nor by *our Works* thereon *His Days*
        profane.
With *Honours* due we must our Neigh-
        bours treat;
And sweetly wish them *Lives* both *Long*   65
        and *Sweet*.
With *Chastity* we must our selves Behave;
And do no *Wrong* in what we get or Save.
Truth we must utter, and Abhor to Lye;
And be *Content*, tho' in Adversity.   70
    [*Exod. XX* 3–17. *Matth. XXI* 1.37,38,39]

16. Them who to be in CHRIST
	thro' *Grace*, Consent,
God brings into His *Gracious Covenant*.
	[*Isa. LV.* 3.]	75
17. The *Baptism* of the Lord, assures
	that we
Both *Wash'd* from *Sin* and *Rais'd* from
	Death, shall be.
	[*Rom. V.* 4,5.]	80
18. To *See* the Lord, we at His *Table* Sitt,
And show that we shall in His *Kingdom*
	eat.
	[1 *Cor. XI.* 26.]
19. *Gods Children* His Good *Promises* Enjoy;	85
And *Good* comes of what *Ill* may them
	annoy.
	[2 *Pet I.*4; *Rom. VIII.*28.]
20. His *Angels* he to them does *Guardians*
	make,	90
And these their *Souls*, at their Depar-
	ture take.
	[*Heb. I.*14.]
21. To *Judge the World*, CHRIST will
	descend at Last;	95
A Righteous *Doom* shall by that *Judge*
	be past.
	[*Acts XVI.* 31.]
22. The *Wicked* shall bear bitter *Pain*
	and *Shame*,	100
With *Wicked Spirits* in Eternal Flame.
The *Godly* shall, with their Great GOD,
	on High,
Reap *Joyes*, High *Joyes*, to all Eternity.
	[*Matth. XXV.* 46.]	105

Part Four: Agricola Verse

Singing at the PLOW.

My *Heart*, how very *Hard* its grown!
    Thicken'd and stiffen'd Clay:
Daily trod by the *Wicked One;*
    Of *Sin* the *Beaten Way.*
An *Heart*, wherein compacted *Weeds*   5
    Of *Diverse Lusts* abound;
No Entrance for the Heavenly Seeds,
    Falling on such a Ground!
O my Almighty SAVIOUR, come;
    Thy *Word*'s a wondrous *Plow:*   10
And let thy SPIRIT drive it home;
    This *Heart*, Oh! Break it so!
Lord, let my *Broken Heart* receive
    Thy Truth with Faith and Love:
May it a Just Reception give   15
    To what falls from Above.
Will my GOD *Plow upon a Rock!*
    Change thou the Soyl, my Lord!
My *Heart* once by thy *Plow-share* broke,
    Will Entertain thy Word.   20

The SOWER a *Singer.*

Give me thy Heart, My SAVIOUR says:
    'Tis what I strive to do.
It's Barren: *Change* it, *Lord*, by Grace,
    A *Fruitful Soyl* into.

[1.] When the *Seed* of thy *Word* is cast   5
    On such a *Beaten Road;*
Let not the *Fruit* of all be lost,
    Nor under Foot be trod.
May't be no *Unattentive* Heart,

111

When There thy Lessons fall;   10
    Let not *Hell's Harpyes* do their part
        To rob me of them all.

[2.] Oh, Do not leave my Heart to be
        An *Unaffected Stone*,
    Where Heavens Eye no *Fruit* will see,   15
        But what will *soon* be gone.
    Let there be found of PIETY
        In me a *Root* so deep,
    As from a vile *Apostacy*
        Will me for ever keep.   20

[3.] *Lord*, Let not *worldly Lusts* and *Cares*
        Thy Work in me annoy;
    Cloak all good *Fruit;* and prove the snares
        That shall my Soul destroy.
    Ye Cursed Thorns I deprecate   25
        All your Entanglements.
    My SAVIOUR, Let not these defeat
        Thy Gospels kind Intents.

[4.] O Glorious CHRIST of GOD, from whom
        Does all my *Fruit* proceed;   30
    Let thy *sweet Influences* come,
        And quicken Thou the *Seed*.
    With *Fruits* make me a *Blessed Field;*
        More precious Things than Gold;
    With *Fruits* of thy Good SPIRIT fill'd, 35
        More than an Hundred fold.

The RAIN gasped for.

O *Father of the Rain*, Look down
    Upon us from on high;
If thy Land be not *Rain'd* upon,
    What *Lives* on it will *Dy*.

Lord of the Clouds; In thee we hope;   5
    Thine all the *Bottels* are;
Except Thou open them, a Drop
    won't fall upon us here.

If thou make Heav'n as *Brass*, and burn
   From thence the groaning Field,   10
Thy Earth will soon to *Iron* turn,
   And no Production yield.

O Let thy Seasonable *Rain*
   Drop *Fatness* on our Soyl;
And grant to most unworthy Man   15
   The *Harvest* of his Toil.

But, O my SAVIOUR, in a Showre
   Of *Righteousness* descend:
Gifts on me, with they SPIRIT poure;
   And *Life* that cannot End.   20

Yea, come upon a World forlorn,
   And with a Quickening *Dew,*
Make thou Mankind, of *Water* born,
   Tho' *Dead*, their *Life* Renew.

In the mean time, thy *Ministers,*   25
As *Clouds*, how *Fat* and *Bright*!
May they upon *Salvations Heirs*
   Distil Things Good and Right.

The *Song* of the SITHE.

O My Long-suffering Lord, I own,
   And thy rich *Patience* praise;
The *Mower,* he has not cut me down;
   I stand; O wondrous *Grace!*

I wait, *O of my Life the GOD!*   5
   I'm waiting for the Stroke.
I see the *Mower:* He's on the Road;
   Soon, soon, I'am overtook!

O that I were in *Safety* got;
   That what I can't Evade   10
I may with Comfort meet, and not
   Be of the *Sithe* afraid.

I do with a *Repenting Heart*
　　To thee, my GOD, Return;
From all my *Idols* I depart,　　　　　　　　　15
　　And for my *Follies* mourn.

To Thee, my SAVIOUR, I Resign,
　　All that belongs to me;
Willing to be entirely *Thine,*
　　And *Heal'd* and *Rul'd* by Thee.　　　　　　20

By Thee to be Redeem'd, and made
　　Righteous and *Holy* too;
And by thy *Counsil* to be led,
　　Thy endless *Glory* to.

Now, Welcome *Sithe;* Come, Do thy worst;　　25
　　Strike; Thou canst do no more,
But fit me to be Lodg'd, I trust,
　　In my GOD's Blessed Floor.

The *Sons* of GOD,
Singing among
The *Trees* of GOD;
Full of Sap, and of *Songs* before Him.

A *Barren Tree!* O, Why, *My Lord,*
　　This *Cumberer* of the Ground;
Why has it not yet heard the Word,
　　The Just Word, *Cut it down!*

'Tis owing, O my SAVIOUR, to　　　　　　　　5
　　thy *Intercession* still,
That I am sav'd and standing so,
　　And not thrown down to Hell.

But from this Time, Oh, let me be
　　A *Tree of Righteousness:*　　　　　　　　10
Fill'd with the *Fruits* of it; A *Tree*
　　Which thou wilt own and Bless.

114

A *Tree* planted and prun'd by GOD;
   Fix'd by His *Water-side:*
The *Fruits* thereof Rich, Sweet, and Good;   15
   And Thou thence *Glorified.*

From the *Forbidden Tree* I am,
   How Poison'd and Undone!
From thence, how dismal Mischiefs came,
   And *Deaths*, in which I groan!   20

But, O my SAVIOUR, By thy *Death*
   Upon a *Tree*, thou art
The *Tree of Life*, to which my Faith
   Flies with a Joyful Heart.

On Thee, *O Tree of Life*, I must   25
   Rejoicing Feed and Live;
Thou'lt me, when fell'd and laid in Dust,
   A *Resurrection* give.

Yea, When below to Mortal Eyes
   I must no more appear,   30
Transplanted to thy *Paradise*,
   I shall still flourish there.

The *Songs* of HARVEST.

Tis not the Till'd, Poor, Lifeless *Earth*
   Which gives me all my Store.
No: Tis my GOD! From *Him* comes forth
   All that has fill'd my Floor.

For what I've gather'd from the Field   5
   Thee, Oh! my GOD I bless.
But, Oh! that I *Fruits* too may yield
   To Him who me does *dress!*

My Soul, with *Gladness* fill'd, and *Food;*
   Returns, what shall be made?   10
In this *Abundance serve* thy GOD,
   In HIM for ever *glad.*

Now in *Obedience* all my Days
  Hard at my Work I'll keep;
Him I'l take pains to please and praise;   15
  Assur'd *That I shall Reap.*

Yea, If I must thro' Sorrows go,
  And *Weeping Eyes* employ;
I'm sure, That they in *Tears* who *Sow*
  At length shall *Reap* with *Joy.*   20

But, Oh, What shall I *Reap* anon!
  What *Eyes* did ever see,
Or to what Man on Earth is known,
  What will the *Harvest* be!

My JESUS, My *Rewarder* Thou   25
  Wilt be; and more than so:
Thou my *Reward* wilt be. And now
  No Higher can I go.

Part Five: Hymns

[The *Mercies* of Almighty God]

The *Mercies* of Almighty God
  To miserable *Me,*
Purchas'd by His most precious Blood,
  Are, Oh! how *Rich* and *Free!*
Mercies, which Answer and Remove
  All my just *Miseries:*   5
Mercies, Well-worth my Praise and Love,
  And *Thankful Sacrifice.*
Behold, *O Gracious Lord,* I do
  Present my self to Thee: 10
No *Beasts,* but my *Own Body* to
  My God, shall *Off'red* be.
A *Body,* by the *Death* of *Thine*
  For *Thee* full dearly Bought,
To *Thee,* with Every Thing of mine,   15
  Is now Sincerely brought.
My Living Body Off'red here
  So does continue Still;
Oh! may it *Live,* Thy *Name* to Fear,
  And still to Do Thy *Will.*   20
May, HOLINESS UNTO THE LORD
  On all I do in *It,*
According to Thy *Holy* Word,
  Be now most Plainly Writ.
May I, the *Pleasing* of *Thee,* make   25
  My daily care *therein,*
And never any *Pleasure* take
  Defil'd with Loathsome *Sin.*
Lord, Let me thus my *Reason* use
  In Off'ring Thee *Thy Own:*   30
'Tis all *Right Reason* I should choose
  To be *Thine, Thine* alone.

Isaiah XXVI.

The Title:
When Moab shall be trodden down,
And in mount Sion rest God's hand,
In that day shall this Song, to God
Be sung all over Judah's land.

The Song

A City of exceeding strength   5
Doth henceforth unto us belong,
And the decreed salvation shall
Like walls and bulwarks keep it strong.

2   Set open then the city gates,
That so the righteous nation   10
That keeps the truths, may enter in
And of it take possession.

3   In perfect peace thou wilt him keep
Whose thoughtful mind is one thee stay'd,
And that because his confidence   15
On thee alone is ever lay'd.

4   Put then your trust upon the Lord
Throughout eternal ages length:
Because the Lord Jehovah is
A Rock of everlasting strength.   20

5   For he brought down high seated ones,
The haughty city he laid low,
He laid it level with the ground,
And it into the dust did throw.

6   The feet of the afflicted man   25
Triumphing trampled it upon,
And it ly'th prostrate under foot,
Foot of the poor and needy one.

7   Uprightness is the Kings high way,
The very road the just did take: 30
The path way of the righteous man
Thou didst for him most even make.

8   Moreover in thy judgments way
Thee, Lord, we longing look't to see:
Our souls desire was to thy name,   35
And to the memory of thee.

9   In evening and in morning prayer
My soul thee earnestly desir'd;
Yea with my spirit in midst of me
I day and night for thee enquir'd.   40
For when thy judgments are display'd
On earth, the worlds inhabitants,
Will lay to heart thy righteous works,
And learn the righteousness of saints.

10   Though for a wicked man there should   45
Bowels of divine pity yearn,
Yet he the way of righteousness
By no means will be brought to learn:
In land of righteousness he will
Still work perverse iniquity,   50
He will not well consider of
Jehovah's glorious majesty.

11   Lord, when thine hand was lifted up
In exhaltation very high,
Lest they should see thine hand, they did   55
Perversely turn away their eye.
But they with blushing shame, shall see
The zeal thou for thy people hast,
And the consuming fire that shall
Thine adversaries wholly wast.   60

12   Jehovah, thou for ever wilt
Safety and peace for us ordain:
For our affairs thou manage didst
And for us all our works maintain.

13   O Lord our God, thou only art   65
Our Lord, yet others besides thee
Have lorded it, and over us
Have exercised tyranny:
But notwithstanding henceforth we
No other lord, save thee will take,   70

And of no other name but thine
From this time will we mention make.

14 Those that opprest us now are dead,
So dead that they shall live no more,
Their ghosts from hence departed are,   75
And none shall them to life restore.
Because thou hast them visited,
And them hast utterly destroy'd.
For ever they are perished
And of all memory made void.   80

15 Jehovah thou the nation
Hast very much increast, increast
Hast thou the nation very much,
Thy glory is made manifest;

That nation which thou hadst remov'd,   85
And far away didst send it forth
By dissipating it unto
The utmost ends of all the earth.

16 O Lord, when they were in distress
They did thee visit with their cryes,   90
And secret prayer they poured out,
When as thou diddest them chastize.

17 Like as a pregnant woman when
Approaching child-birth comes apace
Is pain'd, and in her pangs cry's out,   95
So were we Lord before thy face.

18 We have conceiv'd & have been pain'd,
We have as it were brought forth wind,
The worlds inhabitants fell not
On earth no safety we could find.   100

19 Thy dead shall surely live again,
With my dead corps arise they must;
Awake out of the sleep of death
And sing ye who dwell in the dust:
Because the dew that falls on thee   105
Is like the dew that makes herbs grow

And down from hence with violence
The earth the Rephaims shall throw.

20   Come then, my people, enter in
To chambers that most secret are,   110
And after thee, shut thou the doors
And fasten them with utmost care:
There do thou hide thy self a while,
It will but as a moment be,
And all the indignation will   115
Be wholly passed over thee.

21   Behold the Lord is coming forth
Out of his habitation
To punish their iniquity
The earths inhabitants upon.   120
The earth shall then disclose and show
The bloods in her lay buried,
Her slain shall be expos'd to view
And be no longer covered.

Divine hymns.
[I.]*The Song of the Pardoned.*

Luke VII. 4.7.

THE Sin of my *First Father* is
   Mine, the Just Law doth say,
The Sin of a *Vile Nature,* This
   Doth unto me Convey.

Innumerable Sins I do   5
   Hence madly Perpetrate;
Sins, which the Good I *Have* and *Know;*
   Doth sadly aggravate.

But, O my Precious CHRIST, I see,
   THOU art my *Surety* made: 10
A *Full Obedience* was by Thee
   To Thy Great *Father* Paid.

Thy *Vast Obedience* is by Him
   Now freely Reckon'd mine;
And me doth unto *Life* Redeem   15
   That *Righteousness* of Thine.

O may I *Love* that Glorious One:
   Lord, Thou deserv'st *my Love;*
Such Things *Thy Love* hath for me done,
   Things all my Thoughts above!   20

My God, I *Love* Thee; And I *Grieve*
   That I *Love* Thee no more:
I *Love* Thee, and that I may *Live*
   Thy Praises, I Implore.

[II.] *Good Inferences.*

Rom. VIII. 32,33,34,39.

GOD, in His *Love* to man, don't spare
   His own *Beloved* Son;
But gives Him up, the *Curse* to bear,
   For mans *Redemption.*

Since He hath now for *Sinners* done   5
   That *Greatest Thing,* we know,
On us, He won't count any One
   Too Great, for to bestow.

Gods chosen who now can *Arraign*
   Whom God hath *Justify'd*?   10
And who shall dare Those to *Condemn,*
   For whom His Christ hath *Dy'd*?

Dy'd! Yea, and *Rising* from the *Dead,*
   At the *Right-Hand* of God,
He *Sits* in Glorious Pow'r, to *Plead*   15
   The Merits of His Blood.

Us from such *Love* of God as This,
   A *Love* so Free and Great,

124

In our Lord Jesus Christ, there is
   Nothing shall *Separate*.   20

[III.] *The Lessons of the Gospel.*

From Tit. 2,11,12,13,14.

The *Gospel* of Gods Glorious *Grace*,
Which with News of *Salvation*
Shines every where, *Ungodliness*
And *Worldly Lusts*, bids us to shun.

It bids and binds us, all to take,   5
A *Sober, Righteous, Godly* Way,
And Conscience of *all Duty* make,
While in this *present World* we stay:

Hoping and *Looking* daily for
The *Blessed Promise* of this Word,   10
That the *Great God our Savior,*
Shall come in *Glory: Come O Lord*!

Even JESUS CHRIST, who freely gave
Himself to *Death*, for us, that *we*
Might through Him *Redemption* have   15
From that *Worse* Thing *Iniquitie:*

And *He* Himself, so *Purifie*
A *People*, His *own* Choice, and Rare,
Who *Zealous of Good Works* shall be,
And in that Zeal *peculiar*.   20

[IV.] *Evening Thoughts.*

Phil. I. 21.

Thy CHRIST is now my *Life:* I fly
To CHRIST with an *Enliven'd Faith.*
And now 'twill be my *Gain* to *Dy,*
To CHRIST fetch'd by a *Stingless Death.*

An hymn.
The Right Understanding of much Affliction

Heb. XII. 5,6,11.

The Exhortation of the Lord,
With Consolation Speaks to us;
As unto Children, His Good Word,
We Must Remember, Speaking Thus:

'My Child, when God shall Chasten Thee,   5
'His Chastning do thou not Contemn:
'When Thou His Just Rebukes dost see,
'Faint not, Rebuked under Them.

The Lord with fit Afflictions will,
Correct the Children of His Love;   10
He doth Himself their Father still;
By His most Wise Corrections prove.

Afflictions for the present here
The Vexed Flesh will Grievous call;
But Afterwards there will appear,   15
Not Grief, but Peace, the End of all.

Tried, and Coming forth
as Gold.
A Short HYMN,
To Assist the Pauses of a
SELF-EXAMINATION.
The Trial of a Soul,

Believing.

My Soul, Dost thou a *Precious Christ*
Prize above all, & Place on High?
And on His *Gospel-way to Rest*,
Rest, and with *Purest Hopes rely!*

Repenting.

My Soul, The *Death* of Every *Sin*   5
Dost thou as thy own *Life* pursue!
And welcome any *Bitter Thing*
That will more *Bitter Sin* Subdue?

Loving.

My Soul, To *Know* and *Serve* thy God,
To all things here dost thou prefer?   10
And as a *Brother* Seek the Good
Of all that His dear *Children* are?

Coming into the Covenant
of GOD

LORD, *Sav'd by Grace,* how Rich & Free!
My Quick'ned Soul comes at thy call.
I to Thy COVENANT agree;   15
JESUS, *My Head,* Fulfill it all!

Part Six: Bible Verse

X. COMMANDMENTS.

Worship thou shalt no God but me.
No graven Image make to thee.
The Lords Name take not thou in vain.
The Sabbath do not thou profane.
Yield to thy Parents Honour due.   5
And see that thou no Murder do.
Commit thou no Adultery.
Moreover from all Stealing fly.
No false thing of thy Neighbor say.
And Covet not in any way.   10

THE TEN COMMANDMENTS.

LORD, I should have no Lord, beside
Thee, to be Lov'd, Serv'd, *Glorify'd*.
I should the *Glory* due to Thee,
In *Wayes*, pay that *Appointed* be.

Thy *Name*, Thy *Words*, Thy *Works*, I should,   5
Sacred for *proper Uses* hold.
The *Dayes* which thou made *Sacred* hast,
I should not in *Diversions* wast.

In their *Fit places* every one,
I should with all *Fit Honours* own.   10
That *Life* none may unjustly Lose,
Means I should with all kindness use.

Chast I should be in every *part*,
Yea, *chast* in every *Thought* of Heart.
To *Get* and *Keep* my Worldly *Wealth*,   15
I should commit no sort of *Stealth*.

Truth I should utter and *maintain,*
And no *Good Name* with *Slander* Stain.
With Sweet *content* I should Receive
All the *Wise* God will please to give.   20

Lord, by the *Blood* of CHRIST, I pray,
Save me, who do not thus obey;
And by the *Strength* of CHRIST, from hence,
Sav't, Let me yield Obedience.

A Preparatory Thanksgiving-Song, fetch'd from the Beginning and Conclusion of the Hundred and Third Psalm.

A *Wake,* my Soul, *Awake,* and *Bless*
JEHOVAH the most *Blessed* One:
Bless Him, and His Blest *Holiness*
Let all my *Inward Powers* Own.
The *Glories* of that Lord, my Soul,   5
Confess with *Praises,* just and high;
And His vast *Benefits* Extol
With a most Thankful *Memory.*

Tho' thy *Sins* have His Wrath incurr'd
He does those Horrid *Sins* Forgive;   10
And tho' thy *Sins* have thee procur'd
Diseases, These He does Relieve.
He does from *Deaths* and *Hells* dark place
Thy *Life,* though Forfeited, *Redeem:*
And with Rich Mercies of His *Grace,*   15
Thou art, How Richly! *Crown'd* by Him.

Thy *Mouth* did never Wisely Crave
That *Good,* which He would not afford.
Such *Bowels* is our *Fathers* have,
And *more* than *such* are in the Lord.   20

O ye Bright *Angels,* who transcend
In *Might,* show with your *Might* abroad,
While ye His *Will* and *Voice* attend,

132

The Praise of our *Almighty* God.
Armies of *Angels*, that Obey   25
The *Great* Gods only *Son* and *Heir*,
His *Greatness*, Oh! *Gladly* Display:
You and We, His *Glad Servants* are.

All He has *made*, throughout His whole
Dominion too, Let all Adore   30
Their *Maker*: But, O Thou, my Soul,
Bear part with them for-ever-more.

Appendix A. *Diary* and *Paterna* Verse

High Attainments.

Lord, what shall I return unto Him, from Whom all my mercies flow?

(I) To mee to *live*, it *Christ* shall bee,
For All I do, I'l do for Thee.

(II) My *Quæstion* shall bee oft beside,
How thou mayst most bee glorified!

(III) I will not any creature *love*,   5
But in the *Love* of Thee above.

(IV) *Thy Will* I shall embrace for *mine*,
And every Management of Time
Shall please mee (V.) A *Conformity*
To Thee, shall bee my *Aim* and *Eye*.   10

(VI) *Ejaculations* shall ascend,
Not seldome from mee. (VII.) I'l attend
Occasional Reflections, and
Turn all to Gold that comes to hand.

(VII)[1] And in particular, among   15
My *Cares*, I'll try to make my *Tongue*,
A *Tree of Life;* by speaking all
As bee accountable who seall.

(IX) But *last*, yea, *first*, of all I will
Thy *Son* my *Surety* make, and still   20
Implore Him, that Hee would mee bless
With *Strength*, as well as *Righteousness*.

Psal. 68.19.

Blest bee the Great JEHOVAH who
Doth mee with *Daily Blessings* Load
Thou, with a Saviour, dost Bestow
Salvations on mee, O my God!

Psal. 139. 2, 3, 4.

To Thee my Wayes have all been known;   5
Known all my Words have been to Thee:
Thou know'st my Thoughts; My Faults I own;
May all, thro' Christ, now *pardon'd* bee.

Phil. 1. 21.

Thy CHRIST as now my Life; I fly
To CHRIST with an *enlivened Faith*   10
And *now* twill bee my *Gain* to dy
To CHRIST fetcht by a *stingless Death*.

[Health, Bread, with Life, my God mee sends]

Health, Bread, with *Life,* my God mee sends,
    My *Consort, Father, Friends;*
Employment, with Free *Speech* and *Fame,*
    And *Books* to feed the Same.

For *This,* but most, for thy dear *Son,*   5
    My Thanks are now *begun.*
Help mee, Good God, to *love* and *praise,*
    And *serve* thee all my Dayes.

[Lord, bought by thy All-worthy Blood]

Lord, bought by thy All-worthy Blood,
   Life, worthless I Receive:
Nourish'd with *Health*, and *Peace*, and *Food*,
   Free from just *Plagues*, I *live*.

From thy great *Friendship* I enjoy   5
   Friends that my *Jewels* are;[1]
Mee Thou dost in thy *Church* employ
   And still accept my Prayer.[2]

CHRIST, His *Promise*, is mine;[3]
   His *Angels* are my Guard.   10
I'l my long *Praises* therefore join,
   With Thy good *Angels*, Lord.

[In Peace with God Ly down I Will]

In Peace with God Ly down I Will;
   My quiet Sleep I'l take:
In glad Assurance me to dwell,
   Thou, glorious Lord, wilt make

Or,

In Peace with God Ly down I will;
My Quiet Sleep I'l Thankful take.
In glad Assurance me to dwell,
My Great Redeemer, Thou wilt make.

Sometimes I thus varied it.

In Peace with God, & far from Fear.
I'l now Ly down to Rest;
My God, In thy kind Love and Care,
Safe & forever Blest.

Heb. 11. 17. with Gen. 22. 12

The dearest Lord of <u>Heaven</u> gave
<u>Himself</u> an <u>Off'ring</u> once for me:
The dearest Thing on <u>Earth</u> I have,
Now, Lord, I'l offer unto Thee.
I <u>See</u>, my best Enjoyments here   5
Are <u>Loans</u>, and <u>Flow'rs</u>, and <u>Vanities</u>;
E're well-Enjoy'd they disappear:
Vain <u>Smoke</u>, they pierce and Leave o^e <u>Eyes</u>.
But I <u>Beleeve</u>, O Glorious Lord,
That when I Seem to <u>Lose</u> these <u>Toyes</u>,   10
What's <u>Lost</u>, will fully be Restor'd,
In <u>Glory</u>, with Eternal <u>Joyes</u>.
I do <u>Beleeve</u>, That I and <u>Mine</u>,
Shall Come to <u>Everlasting Rest</u>;
Because, <u>Blest JESUS</u>, We are Thine,   15
And with thy <u>Promises</u> are <u>Blest</u>.
I do <u>Beleeve</u>, That Every <u>Bird</u>
Of Mine, which to the ground shall fall,
Does fall at they Kind <u>Will</u> and Word;
Nor I, nor <u>It</u>, is hurt at all.   20
Now my <u>Beleeving Soul</u> does Hear
This among the Glad <u>Angels</u> told:
<u>I know, Thou dost thy Maker Fear,</u>
<u>From whom thou nothing dost withold.</u>

[I Stript of <u>Earthly</u> Comforts am]

I Stript of <u>Earthly</u> Comforts am;
  <u>Stript</u>, Lett me duely mourn:
<u>Naked</u> from <u>Earth</u> at first I came,
  And <u>Naked</u> I Return.
What, but <u>Gifts</u> from above were They?   5
  GOD <u>gave</u> them unto me.
And now they <u>Take</u> their Flight away,
  <u>Taken</u> by GOD they be.
The Name of my Great GOD, I will
  Forever then Adore;   10
Hee's <u>Wise</u>, and <u>Just</u>, and <u>Sovereign</u> Still,
  And Good forevermore.

137

[AND now to Life Rais'd . . .]

AND now to Life Rais'd by the Heavenly Call,
Henceforth, Vain Idols, I Renounce you all.
   Vile Flesh, Thy raging Lust, & Sordid Ease,
My Winged Soul now shall not Serve & Please.
   False World, Thy Lawes shall be no longer Mine,   5
Nor to thy Wayes my Newborn Soul incline.
   Satan, Thou wilt, I know, my Tempter be,
But thy Temptation shall not govern me.
   Foolish I've been; O Lord, I blush, I grieve;
And Gladly would my Woful Folly Leave.   10
Fain would I Turn to God, but can't alone:
Help, Sovereign Grace, Or it will ne'er be done
To the Great GOD of Heaven I repair,
And Help'd by Heaven thus to Him declare.
   Great GOD, Since to be Mine thou Willing art,   15
Oh! Be thou mine! Replies my Conquered Heart.
To Glorify Thee, Glorious Lord, I Take
For That alone which can me Happy make.
   O FATHER, of all Things Creator Great,
Wilt Thou all Happiness for me Create?   20
   Eternal SON of God, Wilt thou me Save,
That I the Hopes may of a Gods Children have?
   Eternal SPIRIT of God, Poor me Wilt thou
With Spiritual Blessings of all sorts Endow?
   Lord, Ravish'd at thy wondrous Grace, I do   25
These gracious offers now Conform unto.
   O Alsufficient ONE, Wilt thou Supply
My Wants from Stores of Rich Immensity?
Shall boundless Wisdome for my Good Contrive?
And boundless Power yᵉ Fruits of Goodness give?   30
Shall Spotless Holiness on me imprint
An Holy Temper, with thine Image in't?
   Lord, Thy Perfections all I do adore;
And to a Perfect Love my Mind would soar.
   A State of BLISS, according to thy Word,   35
Thou Wilt unto thy Chosen ones afford.
   A State of Blissful Rest and Joy, wherein
Rais'd from the Dead, they shall be freed from Sin.
There bath'd in Rivers of Eternal Joy,
No Sorrowes more shall them at all annoy.   40
GOD shall be All in All; Brought nigh to God,

In Him they shall forever make Abode.
They shall See God; The Beatific Sight!
And their own God shall take in them Delight.
 My Soul, Make now thy Choice. O Say: Is This   45
What thou doest Choose for thy chief Blessedness?
Things of this Present Time I now Refuse;
My Blessed GOD, Thee, Thee, and This, I chuse.
May the Sweet JESUS me to Glory bring,
And be my Glorious Prophet, Priest, & King.   50
 Does the Almighty CHRIST of God, to those
That Will, an Union with Himself propose?
My Lord, I Will! The Will thou didst bestow;
To Thee, Oh, Lett me be United so.
 The full Obedience which my Surety paid   55
To God, may That my Righteousness be made.
A Wretched Sinner would appear in That,
Righteous before ye dreadful Judgment-Seat.
 Show me thy Way, O Lord, Lest that I shou'd
Fall by those Mockers that will me delude.   60
To thy Pure Scriptures-Way I will adhere,
And find the Rule of my Whole Conduct there.
 All the Rebellion of my Heart Subdue;
And for thy Work, O Lord, my Strength Renew.
From thy Vast Fulness lett my Faith derive   65
Strength to do all things, & to Thee to Live.
 May thy Good SPIRIT me Possess, & Fill
With Light and Zeal, to Learn and Do thy Will.
With his Kind Flames may He upon me Sieze,
And keep me alwayes on my Bended knees.   70
May all I am and have, be us'd for Him
Whose is my All, for He did me Redeem.
To Thee, Good SPIRIT, I Lift up my Cries,
That thou Wilt fall upon ye Sacrifice.
 May the Bright ANGELS be my Guardians then; 75
For Thee they'l Guard and Guide ye Sons of Men.
 By Thee assisted, LORD, thus I Consent
Unto they Everlasting COVENANT.

[*I did lift up my Voice to Jah*]

I did lift up my Voice to Jah,
From out of Streightness great;
The Lord an Answer gave to me,
With an enlarged Seat.

The Tabernacles of the Just   5
the Voice of Joy afford,
And of Salvation; strongly works
the right Hand of the Lord,

I shall not dy, but live, and shall
the Works of Jah declare;   10
The Lord did sorely chasten me,
but me from Death did spare.

[Go then, my DOVE . . .]

Go then, my DOVE, but now no longer *mine;*
Leave *Earth,* and now in *heavenly Glory* shine.
Bright for thy Wisdome, Goodness, Beauty here;
Now *brighter* in a more *angelick* Sphære.
JESUS, with whom thy Soul did long to be,   5
Into His *Ark,* and Arms, has taken thee.
Dear *Friends,* with whom thou didst so dearly live,
Feel thy *one Death* to *them* a *thousand* give.
Thy *Prayers* are done; thy *Alms* are spent; thy *Pains*
Are *ended* now, in *endless* Joyes and Gains.   10
    I faint, till thy last Words to Mind I call;
    Rich Words! HEAV'N, HEAV'N WILL MAKE AMENDS FOR ALL.

The Sons of God shouting for Joy at the Arrival
of the *Lord's-day*.

My Saviour's risen from the Dead,
And lives enthron'd Above.
The Price of my Salvation's paid;
My Life is in His Love.

140

With holy Sabbaths and Peace 5
   Hath me victorious Blest.
Lord, bring thou my Holiness,
   To Victory and Rest.

[O Glorious CHRIST of God; I Live]

O Glorious CHRIST of GOD; I live
   In Views of Thee alone.
Life to my gasping Soul, oh! give!
   Shine Thou, or I'm undone.

I cannot live, my GOD, if thou 5
   Enlivnest not my Faith.
I'm dead; I'm lost; oh! Save me now
   from a lamented Death!

My glorious Healer, thou restore
   My Health, and make me whole. 10
But this is what I most implore;
   Oh, for an Healed Soul!

Appendix B. Hand-Written Inscriptions

Oct. 12. 1723.

On my dear *Liza* I this Book
    bestow
That she in Heav'nly piety
    may grow
May she begin on Earth
    betimes to mind
The Heav'n where she will
    all her wishes find
May her young soul become
    the holy spouse
Of the Lord whom her
    Lovely mother chose

[Written on the Title Page of *A Monumental Gratitude*]

Soon as the Muse beheld these lines, She said,
The *Members* are preserv'd: But ah, the *Head*!

Poor Lads! the Storm has whirl'd your Brains around;
And all the *Sense* is ship-wrack'd in the SOUND.

The *Pidgeon Py.* A Poem in Imitation of the *Monumental Gratitude.*

Hark, Stygian Muse; the Noise and discord dire,
Of Heated Ovens, and of Crackling Fire,
While Smoke, and Soot, and falling Sticks of Wood,
And Scattering Coal, and foaming Pidgeons Blood,

With hideous Riot all deform the Floor,   5
Rage, fury, firebrands, bellowing outrage, roar.
Reason and Sense avaunt, the py appears,
And charms at once Touch, Eyes, Nose, Mouth, and Ears.
Fall on, Huzza! Break down the Bulwarks Strong
Let Gravy gush and pidgeons Sprawl along.   10
Salt, pepper, Butter, Marrow, flesh and Bones,
Mix in the Mouth while Spoons encounter Spoons
Forks rush at Forks, and plates on plates resound,
Knives Knives repell, and crust recrackles round.
War, tumult, Havock, Sputt'ring, Out-cries   15
[text indecipherable] * * * * * * * Crickets, *
[text indecipherable] * * of * * * * *
Reach to the roof and [indecipherable] * * the * air
Wine, [indecipherable], beer, their Foamy Fellows all,
Tankards on Tankards flour, and Bowl on Bowl,   20
Impetuous fire, but the [indecipherable] * * worst,
[indecipherable] * Glasses crash, and Broken bottles Burst.
But then my song shall later a Mount remain,
As long as * * the plain.

The Table totters, till the * at once   25
Crash to the Floor in one amazing Bounce.

Appendix C. Cotton Mather's Complete Verse: A Bibliography

The following bibliography is based primarily upon Harold S. Jantz's 1943 edition of *The First Century of New England Verse*. New entries supplementing Jantz's edition are indicated by (N). Entries are chronological and include the verse title, the place and date of original publication, the length of the verse and whether or not it is included in this edition. If a poem is omitted, a brief explanatory note follows. For verse contained in the *Diary* and *Paterna*, the source and date of entry is provided. Complete publication information on all verses is listed in my Textual Notes.

List of Abbreviations

I—Included in this text
O—Omitted from this text
N—New, supplemental listing

1. *A Poem Dedicated to the Memory of the Reverend and Excellent Mr. Urian Oakes.* Boston, 1682. 429 lines. (I)
2. High Attainments. *Diary*, 1683. 22 lines. (I, N)
3. *An Elegy On The Much-to-be-deplored Death of That Never-to-be-forgotten Person, The Reverend Mr. Nathanael Collins.* Boston 1685. 390 lines. (I)
4. [In Peace with God Ly down I Will]. *Paterna*, 1685. 4 lines. (I,N)
5. X. Commandments. Boston, 1691. 10 lines. (I)
6. Epitaph [on Shubael Dummer]. Boston, 1691. 24 lines. (I)
7. Health, Bread, with Life, my God mee sends. *Diary*, 1692. 8 lines. (I)
8. Lord, bought by thy All-worthy Blood. *Diary*, 1692. 12 lines. (I)
9. [I stript of Earthly Comforts am]. *Diary*, 1695. 12 lines. (I)
10. A Preparatory Thanksgiving-Song, fetch'd from the Beginning and Conclusion of the Hundred and Third Psalm. Boston, 1696. 32 lines. (I)
11. [The Mercies of Almighty God] Boston, 1696. 32 lines. (I)
12. *Songs of the Redeemed, A Book of Hymns.* Boston, 1697. (O) No copy is known to have survived. The book was referred to by Samuel Mather in his list of his father's publications.
13. The Song of the Pardoned. Boston, 1700. 24 lines. (I)
14. Good Inferences. Boston, 1700. 20 lines. (I)

144

15. The Lessons of the Gospel. Boston, 1700. 20 lines. (I)
16. Evening Thoughts. Boston, 1700. 4 lines. (I)
17. Little Children Brought unto the Lord Jesus Christ. Boston, 1700. 20 lines. (I)
18. Early Religion. 24 lines. Boston, 1700. (I)
19. The Consent of the Believer unto the Ten Commandments. Boston, 1700. 24 lines. (I)
20. The Lords Prayer. Boston, 1700. 32 lines. (I)
21. The Lord's Day. Boston, 1700. 28 lines. (I)
22. Prayer Encouraged. Boston, 1700. 20 lines. (I)
23. An hymn. The Right Understanding of much Affliction. Boston, 1701. 16 lines. (I)
24. *A Poem of Consolations under Blindness.* Boston, 1701. (O) No copy is known to have survived. Mather refers to the poem in his *Diary,* November, 1701, 1:408.
25. The Body of Divinity Versified. Boston, 1702. 54 lines. (I)
26. [I did lift up my Voice to Jah]. *Diary,* 1702. 12 lines. (I)
27. [Isaiah XXVI]. Boston, 1702. One 4-line verse followed by 124 lines. (I)
28. *Conversion Exemplified.* Boston, 1703. 78 lines. (I)
29. My Satisfaction. Boston, 1703. 16 lines. (I)
30. My Resignation. Boston, 1703. 24 lines. (I)
31. My Resolution. Boston, 1703. 12 lines. (I)
32. Songs in Such a Night. Boston, 1703. 16 lines. (I)
33. My Text Paraphrased, and Faith Exhibited. Boston, 1703, 24 lines. (I)
34. [Go then, my Dove]. Boston, 1703. 14 lines. (I)
35. An Elegy Upon the Death of Mrs. Mary Brown. Boston, 1704. 217 lines. (I, N)
36. The Language of a Soul taken in. Boston, 1704. 38 lines. (I, N)
37. A Lacrymatory; Design'd for the Tears let fall at the Funeral of Mrs. Sarah Leveret. Boston, 1705. 120 lines. (I)
38. The Excellent Wigglesworth, Remembred by some Good Tokens. Boston, 1705. 8 lines. (I)
39. The Consent. Boston, 1705. 48 lines. (I, N)
40. *Good Lessons for Children.* Boston, 1706. (O) No copy is known to have survived. Mather refers to the verse in his *Diary,* March 1705/06, 1:555–6.
41. On the Graves of My Young Brethren. Boston, 1706. 170 lines followed by 8 lines in Latin. (I)
42. Epitaphium (on Fitz-John Winthrop). Boston, 1708. (O) Verse entirely in Latin is not included in this edition.
43. Gratitudinis Ergo. An Essay on the Memory of my Venerable Master, Ezekiel Cheever. Boston, 1703. 210 lines, followed by 44 lines of Latin. (I)
44. Upon the Wars of Europe. Boston, 1710. 10 lines in Latin and English. (O) The authorship of the verse is uncertain; it may be by Samuel Sewall.
45. Soul, when the Worlds Fatigue do make to groan. Boston, 1710. 2 lines (O) Couplets are not included in this edition.
46. The Sons of God shouting for Joy at the Arrival of the Lord's-day. *Diary,* 1711. 8 lines. (I)

47. Tried and Coming forth as Gold. Boston, 1712. 16 lines. (I)

48. His lip dropt language, than sweet Honey, sweeter abundance. Letter, to Samuel Penhallow, Boston, 1713. One line of English hexameter. (O) One-line verse and couplets are not included in this edition.

49. Instructions for Children. Boston, 1713. 104 lines. (I)

50. Epitaphium (on Wait Winthrop). Boston, 1717. 69 lines. (O) Verse entirely in Latin is not included in this edition.

51. *Psalterium Americanum*. Boston, 1718. 410 pages. (O) Complete books of verse are not included in this edition.

52. [On my dear *Liza* I this Book bestow]. Hand-inscribed in a copy of *Co-elestinus*. Boston, 1723. 6 lines. (I, N)

53. Epitaphium (on Increase Mather). Boston, 1724. 137 lines. (O) Verse entirely in Latin is not included in this edition.

54. [O Glorious Christ of God; I live]. *Diary*, 1724. 12 lines. (I)

55. Singing at the Plow. Boston, 1727. 20 lines. (I)

56. The Sower a Singer. Boston, 1727. 36 lines. (I)

57. The Rain gasped for. Boston, 1727. 28 lines. (I)

58. The Song of the Sithe. Boston, 1727. 28 lines. (I)

59. The Sons of God, Singing among the Trees of God; Full of Sap, and of Songs before Him. Boston, 1727. 32 lines. (I)

60. The Songs of Harvest. Boston, 1727. 28 lines. (I)

61. Fleres si scires unum tua tempora Mensem. Boston, 1727. Two-line verse in Latin, followed by a paraphrase in English. (O) Couplets and verse primarily in Latin are not included in this edition.

62. What was conceal'd from thee, O Saint below. Boston, 1728. 2 lines. (O) Couplets are not included in this edition.

63. The Pidgeon Py. A Poem in Imitation of the Monumental Gratitude. Hand-inscribed in a copy of *A Monumental Gratitude*. New London, 1727. Two couplets followed by 26 lines. (I)

Notes

"My Satisfaction."

1. Occasioned by the death of Mather's infant son, Samuel (born 1700, died 1701). Mather had a premonition that his son would die: "[I] live in a continual Apprehension that the Child, (tho' a lusty and hearty Infant) will dy in its Infancy." (*Diary*, January, 1700/01, 1:380.)

"Go then, my Dove"

1. Occasioned by the death of Mather's first wife, Abigail, in 1702, after sixteen years of marriage. It was originally published as an epigram in a book distributed to mourners at her funeral. Mather incorporated his wife's last words into the final line of the poem: "Heav'n, Heav'n will make amends for all." (*Diary*, December, 1702, 1:449–50.)

"A Poem Dedicated to . . . Urian Oakes."

1. Urian Oakes, one-time minister of Cambridge, became president of Harvard College during Mather's sophomore year in 1679; he continued to serve until his death in 1681. Mather's elegy on Oakes, composed at the age of nineteen, was his first published work.

2. Vergilius Maro (Virgil), Roman poet (70–19 B.C.).

3. Allusions to the following elegies written by ministers on the occasion of their fellow ministers' deaths: John Cotton (1584–1652), "On my Reverend and dear Brother, Mr. Thomas Hooker," in posthumous edition of Hooker's *A Survey of the Summe of Church-Discipline* (London, 1648); John Norton (1606–63), "A Funeral Elegie upon the death of the truely Reverend Mr. John Cotton," in Nathaniel Morton, *New Englands Memoriall* (Cambridge, MA, 1669), pp. 136–37; John Wilson (ca. 1588–1667), "Johannes Nortonus," prefixed to John Norton, *Three Choice and Profitable Sermons* (Cambridge, 1664); Jonathan Mitchell (1624–68), "Upon the Death of . . . Mr. John Wilson," in Nathaniel Morton, *New Englands Memoriall*, pp. 185–88; Thomas Shepard (1635–77) may have written an elegy on Jonathan Mitchell, but if so, it has not survived; Urian Oakes, *An Elegie upon The Death of . . . Thomas Shepard* (Cambridge, 1677).

4. Icharus, in Greek mythology, son of Daedalus who flew so close to the sun that the heat melted his wax wings, causing him to fall to his death.

5. Ahimaaz, son of Ahinoan, wife of Saul (I. Sam. 14:50).

6. Tiberius, Roman emperor (A.D. 14–A.D. 37).

7. Absalom, third son of David.

8. Mather may be alluding to Lucius Licinius Crassus, Roman orator and politician (140–91 B.C.).

9. Ephialtes, traitor who reputedly guided a Persian detachment up mountain paths to the Pass of Thermopylae in 480 B.C.

10. *Mr.* M. Wigglesworth, *in Pref. to* D. D. [Mather's note].

11. Elisha, son of Shaphat, successor to Elijah, and prophet of the Northern Kingdom of Israel.

12. Jeremiah is called Jeremy in the New Testament.

13. Josiah, son of Amon, King of Judah, and Jedidah, daughter of Adaiah of Boscath. He became king at the age of eight, succeeding his father who had been murdered by his henchmen.

14. Hadad-rimmon, the combination of Syrian Gods Hadad (a rain god dwelling in the North Syrian mountains) and Rimmon (a storm god symbolized by a thunderbolt).

15. Memories.

16. the Past.

17. Probably an allusion to the following: Alexander Whitaker (1585–1617), minister who baptized Pocahontas and drowned in 1617 while crossing the James River in Virginia; William Perkins (1558–1602), English Puritan theologian; and John Preston (1587–1628) master of Emmanuel College, Cambridge, and author of *A Treatise on the Covenant.*

18. *Non Annis, sed Factis vivunt mortales.* [Mather's note]. Not with years, but with deeds do mortals live.

19. An allusion to Thomas Fuller (1608–61), author of *History of the Worthies of England* (1662).

20. Saint Ambrose (340?–397), served as Bishop of Milan and worked for relief of the poor.

21. Hiram, King of Tyre (970–936 B.C.), friend of Solomon and David.

22. Bezaleel, divinely inspired craftsman, teacher, and architect, (Ex. 31:1–5, 35:34, and 36, 37, 38).

23. Roxbury, Massachusetts, Oakes's first pastorate.

24. Oakes returned to Tichfield, England, in 1654 to assume a ministry there.

25. Probably an allusion to Mt. Ebal, where Joshua built a stone altar inscribed with a pronouncement to Israel of curses that would befall it if breaches of covenant law were made; henceforth, it was known as the Mount of Cursing.

26. Probably Richard Sibbs (1577–1635), eminent English Puritan minister.

27. *Pralucendo pereo.* [Mather's note]. By lighting the way I am lost.

28. Possibly a reference to one of the twelve apostles.

29. *Col. N.* [Mather's note]. The cryptic nature of Mather's note makes his reference nearly impossible to identify.

30. Obadiah, minor Hebrew prophet of uncertain date whose judgment on Edom, for siding with Israel's enemy, is recorded in the Old Testament.

31. Obed-Edom, a man from Gath in whose care David left the ark for three months before transporting it to Jerusalem.

32. Edward Symmons, English minister and author of four sermons addressing ecclesiastical self-seeking published in London (1642).

33. Jonathan Mitchell (1624–68), influential Puritan minister who served for eighteen years as pastor of the church in Cambridge, Massachusetts.

34. Sir Thomas More (1478–1535) sketched a Latin description of the imaginary island of Utopia, (*Utopia*, [1516]), which advocated communal ownership of land, education for both men and women, and religious toleration.

35. Probably an allusion to William Twiss (1575–1646), English nonconformist divine.

36. An allusion to St. John Chrysostom (345?–407), known for his eloquence. Mather routinely compared the subjects in his writings to well-known historical figures. His purpose in doing so was two-fold: to emphasize the greatness of the subjects about whom he wrote and to remind his readers of the importance of their mission in the New World. For a fine discussion of this device, see William R. Manierre's "Cotton Mather and the Biographical Parallel" in *American Quarterly* 13 (Spring 1961): 153–60.

37. Pope Pius II (1405–64), eminent historian and scholar.

38. Capernaum, a small lake port on the northwest shore of the Sea of Galilee.

39. An intermittent fever that recurs at approximately 72-hour intervals.

40. Orestes, son of Agamemnon who murdered his mother and her lover, thus avenging the murder of his father.

41. *Mr.* Charles Chauncey. *B. D.* [Mather's note]. Chauncey (1592?–1672) was president of Harvard College from 1654 until his death.

42. Possibly meaning barren or dry; from the word gast.

43. of sorrows.

44. Probably an allusion to Baron Arthur Capel, member of the British Parliament, who was executed in 1649.

45. *Hinc Illæ Lachrymæ*! [Mather's note]. Hence These Tears!

46. Probably on allusion to Johann Jacob Grynæus (1540–1617), Swiss theologian and author.

47. *O faelicens Diem! quum ad illud Animarum Concilium proficiscar; et ex hac Turba & Colluvione dif. cedam.* [Mather's note].

48. John Dod (1547–1645), English Puritan divine.

49. Heinrich Bullinger (1504–75), Swiss reformer and disciple of Zwingli.

50. Theodorus Beza (1519–1605), French Protestant theologian, who with Calvin became leader of the French Reformation.

51. Briareus, a giant monster with (traditionally) a hundred arms, the offspring of Uranus and Gaia.

52. Cic. *pro* hic *Poetæ.* [Mather's note]. Cicero on behalf of this poet.

53. Mephiboshoth, son of Jonathan and grandson of Saul, lamed as a child (II Sam. 4:4).

54. Both Jan Drusius (1550–1616), and his son Jan Drusius (1588–1609) excelled in Hebrew. The elder Drusius was a professor of oriental languages at Oxford, England from 1572–77. He wrote commentaries on Scripture and several treatises on grammar. The younger Drusius addressed the King of England in a Latin oration at the age of seventeen.

55. *See the parallel in Mr.* Mather's *Epistle before a late* Sermon *of Mr.* Oakes. [Mather's note].

56. A man of his name.

57. Urianus *quasi* [unreadable in original]. [Mather's note].

58. In his youth St. Augustine studied at Carthage, devoting his time to Latin poets.

59. *So stiled by Mr.* Burroughs. [Mather's note]. Possibly an allusion to George Burroughs (1650?–92), New-England clergyman.

60. Mather presents Oakes as a model worthy of emulation for a tyro (a beginner).

61. Aliquis *in Omnibus,* Nullus *in Singulæ.* [Mather's note]. Someone in

everyone, no one in each of them.

62. Orpheus, famous musician and son (or pupil) of Apollo.

63. Cf. Collins note 78 below.

64. Cf. Collins note 77 below.

65. A wise old counselor who fought with the Greeks at Troy.

66. the bosom of Abraham.

67. I shall speak.

68. I have spoken.

69. Ichabod, son of Phinehas and grandson of Eli, born during the capture of the Ark by the Philistines.

70. An allusion to the first oasis reached by the Children of Israel, after they crossed the Sea of Reeds.

71. *ANAGR.* [Mather's note].

72. *ANAGR.* [Mather's note].

73. Mr. *OAKES's* Elect. Serm. [Mather's note]. In 1673, Oakes preached a sermon entitled "New-England Pleaded with."

74. The name of a child whose birth Isaiah predicted to Ahaz during the Syro-Ephriamitic war as a sign meaning "God is with us."

75. The fertile land assigned to the Israelites in northeast Egypt.

76. Hephzibah, another name for Jerusalem.

77. Name given to Palestine after the exile when it repopulated and was restored to God's favor.

78. The Latin may be translated:

Many brave men lived before Agamemnon; but all, unlamented and unknown, are weighed down by a long night, because they lack a sacred poet. (Horace)

I do not desire to embrace all things in my verses. (Virgil)

He shall praise the long poem: He shall read the short! (Calliope)

You who read those things if you praise everything of mine improve your stupidity: if nothing, your envy. (Owen)

Many erasures cannot, Reader, improve these our verses. One erasure can. (Martial)

"An Elegy on . . . the Reverend Mr. Nathanael Collins"

1. Nathanael Collins, pastor of the church of Middletown, Connecticut, was born in Cambridge, Massachusetts, on 7 March 1643. He earned both his B.A. and M.A. from Harvard College. He was a close friend of Mather's, who mourned his early death on 28 December 1684.

2. *Isai.* 57.1 [Mather's note].

3. *allusion to the poetical fancy of Ajax* [Mather's note]. Ajax, powerful Greek warrior, famous for the great shield he carried.

4. *Dorcas, Act.* 9.39. [Mather's note].

5. *Psa.* 112.6 [Mather's note].

6. *whom the Roman conspirators* [followed by several unreadable words] [Mather's note].

7. *Gen.* 50.2. [Mather's note].

8. *all. to* 2. *King.* 2.12. [Mather's note].

9. *so some render* the Garden of Nuts, *Cant.* 6.11. *in a phrase very accommodable to* America. [Mather's note].

10. *Cant.* 1.7. [Mather's note].

11. *some (tho' groundlesly though) suppose a* Church *intended by that* name *in* 2. *Joh.* 1. [Mather's note].

12. *all. to the* figure *thereof in* B. K.'s *ingenious poem.* [Mather's note]. The cryptic nature of Mather's note makes the poet nearly impossible to identify.

13. *Mat.* 2.18. [Mather's note].

14. *viz. the Canticles.* [Mather's note].

15. *all. to such a* metamorphosis *celebrated in Ovid.* [Mather's note].

16. *Hinc illa lacrymæ.* [Mather's note]. Hence these tears.

17. *fuimus Troes.* [Mather's note]. We were Trojans.

18. Possibly an allusion to Cornelius Loos (1545?–95), a Dutch theologian who was persecuted for condemning the practice of burning witches.

19. *Lam.* 1.1. [Mather's note].

20. *Eccles.* 7.1. [Mather's note].

21. *from whose corpse 'tis said there went a* smell *surprizingly fragrant.* [Mather's note].

22. *praised by* Pichennerus, [Mather's note]. The identity of Mather's source is unclear.

23. *praised by* Huttenus, [Mather's note]. Probably an allusion to Ulrich von Hutten (1488–1523), humanist and writer who supported Luther's cause in the Reformation. Attacked by Rome and abandoned by Erasmus, his writings became more threatening and inflammatory. Hutten took refuge in Zurich, where Zwingli took care of him until his early death.

24. *praised by* Glaucus, [Mather's note]. Probably an allusion to the mythological son of Sisyphus, who leaped into the sea in grief.

25. *praised by* Erasmus, [Mather's note]. An allusion to Desiderius Erasmus (1466?–1536), Dutch scholar and theologian who taught Greek at Cambridge and was regarded as a leader of the Renaissance in northern Europe.

26. *praised by* Pierius, all in set poems, or orations. [Mather's note]. An allusion to Pierius, the martyr, who appears to have headed the catechetical school at Alexandria.

27. *as once a humoursome person did.* [Mather's note].

28. Socrates, *who spent* 15 *year in framing of one* Panegyric, *one oration.* [Mather's note].

29. Apelles, Greek painter of fourth century B.C., often regarded as the greatest painter of antiquity.

30. *as that painter did upon his Minerva's.* [Mather's note].

31. *of which I can with my* Microscope *see incredible hundreds playing about in one drop of water.* [Mather's note].

32. *which* speaking-Trumpet *may be heard a vast way off* [Mather's note].

33. *all to* ye Acrost. of Mors *Mordens Omnia Restro Suo.* [Mather's note]. Death devouring everything.

34. Tit. Vesp. *who was termed,* Deliciæ *humani generis.* [Mather's note]. Titus Vespasianus (A.D.39?–81), Roman emperor and general who was termed delight of the human race.

35. *v. the glorious catalogue* 2 *Pet.* 1.5,7. [Mather's note].

36. 2. *Cor.* 4.18 [Mather's note].

37. *whose saying often was,* Amor meus est crucifixus [Mather's note]. My love has been crucified.

38. *which is grosly and fabulously reported of another.* [Mather's note].

39. *two glories of the heathen, the one for* Justice, *the other for* Fidelity. [Mather's note].

40. Marcus Atilius Regulus, Roman hero tortured to death around 250 B.C.

41. *Act.* 7.22. [Mather's note].

42. *Exod.* 34.35. [Mather's note].

43. *Prov.* 15.4. [Mather's note].

44. *golden mouth.* [Mather's note].

45. *as in Exod.* 32.10. feriendi licentiam petit a *Mose* qui fecit *Mosen.* [Mather's note]. He who made Moses sought liberty of punishing from Moses.

46. *preces et lacrymæ sunt Arma Ecclesiæ.* [Mather's note]. Prayers and tears are the arms of the Church.

47. *Psa.* 90.12. [Mather's note].

48. *and an* invisible point *no doubt would it be to an* humane eye *in the* starry Heaven, *tho it probably contains above* Ten Thousand Millions *of cubic German* leagues. [Mather's note].

49. *as some other Philosophy is call'd in* Col. 2.8. [Mather's note].

50. presentem docuit quælibet herba Deum. [Mather's note]. Any blade of grass shows that God is present.

51. *Socrates* his *Hoc tantum scio, me nihil scire.* [Mather's note]. This only I know, that I know nothing.

52. *the* Pleasures, *and* Profits & Honours *of the world, become the* 3 Belzebubs *of it, according to the Distich*

Ambitiosus honos et opes et fæda voluptas,
Hæc tria pro trino Numine mundus habet.

[Mather's note].

Ambitious honor and riches and coarse desire,
These three the earth holds for the three divinities.

53. *Dan.* 1. 12. [Mather's note].

54. *Jer.* 35.6. [Mather's note].

55. *Mat.* 3.4. [Mather's note].

56. *Psa.* 119.62. [Mather's note].

57. *K. Edw.* VI. *us'd to call the Princess* Elizabeth, *his* Sister Temperance. [Mather's note].

58. *It was the sentence of a great Saint under great pain,* I groan but do not grumble. [Mather's note].

59. *whom* Homer *so often represents in fumes.* [Mather's note].

60. *as was wont to do the Renowned* Roman Emperour. [Mather's note].

61. *allusion to* Sola fit humanæ pietas cynosura carinæ. [Mather's note]. Piety alone becomes the constellation of the human ship.

62. Amo te. Domine, plusquam meos, plusquam mea, plusquam me. *Bern.* [Mather's note]. I love you Lord, more than my family, more than my possessions, more than myself.

63. *all. to* Rom. 6.17. gr. [Mather's note].

64. *as he,* Propter te, Domine, propter te. [Mather's note]. Because of you, Lord, because of you.

65. *of whom Ecclesiastical History relates, that his* hardned knees wore *the Badges of his* hard prayers [Mather's note].

66. *as Jerome remarkt of his friend* Nepotian. [Mather's note].

67. *Anima justi Cælum est.* [Mather's note]. The soul of justice is the sky.

68. *prov.* 31.26. [Mather's note].

69. *which name signifies* brotherly love. *Heb.* 13.1. *gr.* [Mather's note].

70. *of whom tis said that when through age he could do no more, he would give that short Lesson for a* long Sermon *to his congregation,* my Children, love one another. [Mather's note].

71. *a savory speech recorded of the famous* Zwinglius. [Mather's note].

72. Thomas Cranmer (1489–1556), Archbishop of Canterbury, burned at the stake for treason.

73. *Holy Mr.* Fox. [Mather's note]. An allusion to George Fox (1624–91) English religious leader and founder of the Society of Friends.

74. *Seneca.* [Mather's note].

75. Possibly an allusion to Marcus Porcius Cato (234–149 B.C.), Roman statesman who endeavored to restore by legislation what he believed to be the high morals and simplicity of life characteristic of the early days of the republic.

76. Ille pius pastor, quo non prestantior unus, Qui faciendo docet, quæ facienda docet. [Mather's note]. That pious pastor, whom no one is more distinguished than, who learned by doing, learns what must be done.

77. Probably an allusion to Barnabas, a Levite of Cyprus who sold his land and donated the proceeds to the early church.

78. Christ's appellation of apostles James and John, explained as "sons of thunder."

79. *all. to* 2. Cor. 2.17. *gr.* [Mather's note].

80. *all. to those 2 creatures in Rev.* 4.7. *whereof by the former some will have the* Pastor, *& by the latter the* Teacher *of a* Church *to be meant.* [Mather's note].

81. Mt. Pisgah, a headland of the Abarim range in Jordan, prized for its springs in ancient times. The aged Moses had a panoramic view of the Promised Land from the mountain.

82. *so* Alexander Hales. [Mather's note]. Alexander of Hales (?–1245), English theologian and author of *Summa Theologiae.*

83. *so* Bradwardine. [Mather's note]. Thomas Bradwardine (1290?–1349), English prelate and mathematician. He was chaplain and confessor to Edward III and Archbishop of Canterbury in 1349.

84. *so* Scotus. [Mather's note]. Duns Scotus (1265?–1308), who was known as Doctor Subtilis because of his dialectical skill and refined distinctions. He founded a scholastic system called Scotism.

85. *so* Aquinas. [Mather's note].

86. *thus distinguished in an* Epigram of Beza's [Mather's note].

87. Guillaume Farel, leader in the French Reformation who persuaded Calvin to settle in Geneva.

88. Viret (1511–71), Swiss reformer converted to Protestantism by Farel in 1531.

89. *whose tenacious* Memory *is to all Ages* memorable. [Mather's note].

90. *all. to Act* 16.14. [Mather's note].

91. *an excellent Divine, the English of whose Name seems to be* Key-carrier: [Mather's note].

92. *another, whose Name in likelyhood was* House-Lamp. [Mather's note].

93. Johannes Oecolampadius (1482–1531), German theological leader in the Swiss Reformation.

94. *observing the* Motto *of the Emperour* Severus, *wkich was* LABOREMUS. [Mather's note]. Observing the motto of Roman emperor L. Septimus Severus (A.D.193–211) which was let us work hard.

95. *all. to Cant.* 4.1. *where by those expressions some understand* Christian Teachers *surrounded with their* believing Hearers. [Mather's note].

96. *One of his last Services was that he assisted in a* Day of Prayer at *New-Haven, immediately on which he sickned.* [Mather's note].

97. *He died on a* Sabbath Day *about the beginning of* the Morning Exercise. [Mather's note].

98. *about* 44. [Mather's note].

99. *Immodicis brevis est ætas et rara senectus.* [Mather's note]. For the unrestrained a lifetime is brief and old age rare.

100. Micaiah, a prophet of Israel, was sentenced to prison because of an unpleasant forecast. His final fate is unknown.

101. 1. *King.* 22.17. [Mather's note].

102. *allusion to Psal.* 87.5. [Mather's note].

103. *all. to* Isai. 5. [Mather's note].

104. An allusion to David Waengler Pareus (1548–1622), Heidelberg Protestant theologian and advocate of toleration and conciliation among Lutherans, Calvinists, and Anglicans.

105. An allusion to the Heidelberg Catechism, published in 1563 at Heidelberg, Germany. The catechism was written to restore harmony in the churches during the Reformation.

106. An allusion to St. Augustine, Bishop of Hippo.

107. 2. *King.* 15.20. *'Tis one of the Jewish Oracles,* Quando Luminaira patiuntur Eclipsin, malum est signum mundo. [Mather's note]. When the windows suffer an eclipse, it is an evil sign for the world.

108. *Some have observed,* that the *Death* of a faithful *Minister* in a place where he hath done God much service, is oft attended with a great Mortality among other persons in that place. *I. Collins. Elijahs Lamentation, p.* 18. [Mather's note].

109. *See Amos* 8.11. [Mather's note].

110. *A Bird fam'd for its regard to its Dam.* [Mather's note].

111. *One of the most splendid Cities wherein, is hence appositely term'd* Lutetia. [Mather's note].

112. *Vitam habentes in* patientia, *Mortem in* desiderio. [Mather's note]. Holding life in resignation, death in desire.

113. *See Jer.* 22.17.

114. Jehoiakim, King of Judah in Jerusalem, whose bold irreverence displayed itself in the manuscript-burning incident described in Jer. 36:1–26.

115. *v.*2. Sam. I.17. [Mather's note].

116. *all. to the* Mare mortuum. [Mather's note]. Allusion to the dead sea.

117. *such the* Jews *were wont to have at their* Funerals. [Mather's note].

118. *all. to Luk.* 23.28. [Mather's note].

119. *all. to Phil.* 1.23. *where to* depart, *is by some translated* to loose Anchor. [Mather's note].

120. Mors Beatitudinis principium, Laborum meta, peremptoria peccatorum, *Aug.* [Mather's note]. Death is the beginning of blessedness, the goal of hardships, the destruction of sins.

121. *Christ & his* Cross *part at Heavens door, for there's no room for* Crosses *in Heaven.* Rutherf. Epist. [Mather's note].

122. *Caini adhuc clavus Abelis sanguine rubens ubique circumfertur.* Bucholtz. [Mather's note]. Thus far the club of Cain red with the blood of Abel was carried around everywhere.

123. *The Heaven of Heaven, pourtray'd in Joh.* 17.24. [Mather's note].

124. *skil'd in the language which bold conjectures think to be* Heavens Dialect. [Mather's note].

125. One versed in Hebrew; a Hebrew scholar.

126. *all.* to 2 *Cor.* 4.7. gr. [Mather's note].

127. *the territories whereto the apostate troops of Lucifer seem to be confined, from Eph.* 2.2. [Mather's note].

128. *all.* to 1 Cor. 5.5. [Mather's note].

129. *all. to* 2. *ibid. where an* upper garment of glory *is engaged to the souls on which an* under garment *of* grace *is wrought with the Eternal Spirits* Needlework. [Mather's note].

130. *v. Joh.* 1.47. [Mather's note].

131. *a thing rationally sung by the* German Swan *the night before he died.* [Mather's note].

132. *a line purposely* too long *for the verse, but too short not* [several words in original unreadable] *shaddow of* ETERNITY. [Mather's note].

133.

> May it befall me thus to live and thus to die
> Thus he desires,
> Who always worshipping follows far the footsteps.
> Such a life, thus.

"An Elegy Upon . . . Mary Brown;"

1. Mary Brown, a devout parishioners of Mather's, died in childbirth on 26 December 1703. Mather stated in his diary that he composed this long elegy "to make Poetry subservient unto the Designs of Vertue." (*Diary*, December 1703/04, 1:501).

2. An allusion to a violent, wanton, insolent man, derived from the Greek word "hybristikos."

3. Plutarch (A.D. 46?–120?), Greek biographer and historian.

4. Probably an allusion to Johann Heinrich Hottinger (1620–67), Swiss Protestant theologian and orientalist.

5. Saint Agatha, a virgin martyr of Sicily in the middle of the third century.

6. Saint Eulalia, a Christian martyr born at Merida, Spain about A.D. 290, who perished at the stake under the reign of Maximian, at about age fourteen.

7. An allusion to greed and worship of material wealth.

8. Philo of Judaeus (20 B.C.–A.D. 50), greatest philosopher of Hellenistic Judaism who left his mark on Christian theology. One of his outstanding contributions was his use of allegory by which he turned biblical stories into philosophical principles.

9. The allusion to Herpine is probably the result of a typesetter's error. The correct word appears to be Heroine.

10. Possibly an allusion to Porcia (sometimes Portia), a Roman matron eminent for her magnanimity, prudence, and fortitude. She inflicted a wound on herself to prove she was worthy to be the confidante of her husband in respect to affairs of state.

11. Possibly an allusion to Tertullus, the prosecuting attorney who made a charge against Paul, castigating him as a pestilent fellow who provoked sedition among Jews throughout the world.

12. Herod Agrippa II (A.D. 27–A.D. 93), son of Herod Agrippa I and Cypros, who authorized the famous statement of defense spoken by Paul (Acts 26) after which the king uttered his notable words: "Almost thou persuadest me to be a Christian."

13. Nicholas Noyes, contemporary of Mather, minister and poet whose own elegy on Mary Brown followed Mather's in *Eureka. The Vertuous Woman found.*

14. An allusion to the virtue of prudence found in numerous biblical passages.

15. The Ten Commandments.

16. Probably an allusion to James Durham (1622–58), eminent Scotch divine of the seventeenth century who wrote numerous essays on religion including "An Exposition of the Commandments."

17. Son of the Earth.

"A Lacrymatory; Design'd for the Tears let fall at the Funeral of Mrs. Sarah Leveret."

1. Sarah Leveret, wife of John Leveret, Governor of Massachusetts from 1673 until 1679, died in 1704–5 at the age of seventy-five.

2. Mather's allusion is unclear.

3. Huldah, a reputable prophetess and wife of Shallum, the wardrobe keeper (2 Kings 22:14).

4. Probably an allusion to Hypatia, a Greek philosopher celebrated for her beauty, killed by a mob in A.D. 415.

5. Eudoxia (?–A.D. 404), empress of the Eastern Roman Empire who controlled her husband Arcadius and sent John Chrysostom into exile for preaching against her wickedness.

6. Probably an allusion to Heribert Rosweide (1569–1629), Dutch Jesuit, who in 1615 wrote "Vitæ Patrum, sive Historia eremitica" (Lives of the Fathers).

7. Sirius, the dog star in the constellation Canis Major, called the brightest star in the heavens, which the ancients thought caused excessive heat on earth, resulting in scorched and barren fields.

8. Cassiopea's Chair, the most conspicuous group of stars in the constellation Cassiopea, the outline of which resembles a chair.

9. Cf. Collins note 105 above.

"On the Graves, of My Young Brethren."

1. The seven ministers Mather alludes to are: John Clark (1670–1705), minister at Exeter, New Hampshire, from 1693 until his death at the age of thirty-five; Andrew Gardner (1674–1704), pastor at Lancaster, Massachusetts, shot and killed at the age of thirty during an attack by Indians; John Hubbard (1677–1705), minister at Jamaica, Long Island, from 1702 until his death at the age of twenty-eight; John Morse (1674–1700), minister at Newtown, Long Island, until his death at the age of twenty-six; Edward Thompson (1665–1705), minister at Marshfield, Massachusetts, from 1696 until his death at the age of forty; John Wade (1674/5–1702), ordained as first pastor of the church at Berwick, Maine, just a few months before his death at the age of twenty-eight; and Jabez Wakeman (1678–1704), minister at Newark, New Jersey, at the time of his death at age twenty-six during an outbreak of dysentery. Only Hubbard and Clark are mentioned by name in this elegy; the other five ministers are addressed in the essay preceding the poem.

2. Because they lack a sacred poet.

3. A family of Jewish patriots who, under Judas Maccabaeus, headed a successful revolt against the Syrians and ruled Palestine until 37 B.C.

4. Justinian (A.D. 483–565), ruler of the Eastern Roman Empire.

5. An allusion to the town of Debir, conquered by Joshua.

6. Antoninus Pius (A.D. 86–161), Roman emperor who, succeeding Hadrian, dispensed nine liberalities.

7. John Asgill (1659–1738), English lawyer noted for a 1700 treatise which sought to prove that because the penalty for original sin had been paid by Christ, death was no longer legal and Christians would thus pass to eternity by "translation." His actions caused his expulsion from the House of Commons on the grounds of blasphemy.

8. Guido Panciroli (1523–99), Italian lawyer, antiquarian, and author.

9. Severus Cassius (?–A.D. 34), brilliant Augustan orator.

10. St. Basil (A.D. 329–379), supporter of the orthodox faith against Arianism and author of scriptural commentaries, liturgies, and homilies.

11. Plutarch (A.D. 46–120), author of biographies of Greek and Roman soldiers and statesmen.

12. Thetis, a sea goddess, mother of Achilles.

13. Probably an allusion to Merope, one of seven daughters of Atlas and Pleione, who surrendered her immortal nature by marrying a mortal.

14. From the Panegyric of Paulinus on the Death of Celsus.

The Latin may be translated:

> Oh what shall I do? With wavering piety I am troubled considering,
> Should I give thanks or grieve? The boy is deserving of both.
> Love for him moves me to tears and joy;
> But Faith orders me to rejoice, Piety to weep.
> So moderate a profit from so sweet a pledge
> I bewail in the small extent of time has been given to the fathers.
> I rejoice that he, who suffered his mortal trials in a brief lifetime, died.
> That he might quickly obtain divine riches.

"Gratitudinis Ergo. An Essay on the Memory of my Venerable Master, Ezekiel Cheever."

1. Ezekiel Cheever was born in England in 1616 and served as schoolmaster in various New-England settlements before settling in Boston in 1670. Mather's admiration of the instruction he received from Cheever is amply illustrated in the elegy. Cheever died in Boston in 1708 at the age of ninety-four.

2.

> To bind with an august song praises,
> Which no power of eloquence is able to honor.

3. Kenneth Silverman, in *Colonial American Poetry,* suggests that perhaps Mather is alluding to Saint Sebastian.

4. Teacher.

5. Good.

6. Amo.

7. Of Sorrow.

8. Marcus Tullius Cicero (106–43 B.C.), Roman orator, statesman, and philosopher.

9. Terence (185–159 B.C.), Roman playwright and master of Latin comedy.

10. Greek folly.

157

11. Elijah Corlet (1610–87), master of the Grammar School in Cambridge, Massachusetts, for forty years.

12. A group of picturesque islands southwest of Cornwall, England.

13. A concubine of Abraham and slave of his wife Sarah.

14. William Lily (ca. 1460–1522), whose *Eton Latin Grammar* text was commonly used in schools.

15. Cf. Collins note 75 above.

16. In his youth, St. Augustine studied at Carthage, devoting his time to Latin poets.

17. Dido, famous queen of Carthage who stabbed herself on her funeral pyre.

18. Cf. Oakes note no. 65 above.

19. Angel of good.

20. Ambrosius Theodosius Macrobius, Latin grammarian of the late 4th and early 5th century A.D.

21. John Davenport (1597–1670), founder of the New Haven Colony.

22. iron.

23. Origen (A.D. 185?–254?), one of the most famous of the ancient Christian theologians.

24. And make a sepulchral mound, and add upon the mound a song. (Virgil)

25. The Latin may be translated:

Epitaph

Ezekiel Cheever
Schoolmaster

First of New-Haven;
Then of Ispwich;
After of Charlestown
Last of Boston
whose
Learning and Virtue
You know, if you be a New Englander,
You honor, if you be not a foreigner;
GRAMMARIAN,
from whom talk is not only pure but
also pious;
RHETORICIAN
from whom speech is elegant
not only to men in public
but he also showers
Most effective speeches on God in public
POET
from whom not only songs are composed
But he also
Sings Celestial hymns and angelic odes,
They learn,
Who wish to learn;
A LAMP
for whom has been kindled
Who can count
How many lights of the Churches?
AND
He carried off the corpus of Theology with him

Most experienced THEOLOGIAN,
He placed his own body less dear to him.
He lived 94 years.
He taught 70 years.
He died in 1708 A.D.
And because he is able to die,
He awaits and desires
The first resurrection of the holy ones
for Immortality.
Honor is owed first Immortality.

"Epitaph" [on Shubael Dummer]

1. Occasioned by the death of Shubael Dummer, pastor at York, Maine, shot to death by Indians during a raid in January 1691/2.
2. Elisha, son of Shaphat and prophet of the Northern Kingdom of Israel.

"The Excellent Wigglesworth . . ."

1. Occasioned by the death of Michael Wigglesworth, pastor, physician, and poet of Malden, Massachusetts, who was born in England and died in Malden in 1705. He is best known for his influential poem, "The Day of Doom," through which successive generations of New Englanders were instructed in piety, by the devices of fire and brimstone, before the Revolution.

"High Attainments."

1. Error for VIII.

["Lord, bought by thy All-worthy Blood"]

1. Originally the line read, "*Friends* greatly dear to mee:" [Mather's note].
2. Originally written, "To *speak* and *write* for Thee." [Mather's note].
3. Originally written, "Christ and his promises are mine." [Mather's note].

Textual Notes

"The Body of Divinity Versified."

Source: *Much In a Little*, Boston, 1702. Evans #1071, Jantz #25.

Collated against (A.) "Acceptable Words of Truth," in *Maschil, Or, the Faithful Instructor*, Boston, 1702. Evans #1069, Jantz #25; (B). "The Body of Divinity Versified," in *Cares about the Nurseries*, Boston, 1702. Evans #1065, Jantz #25; (C.) "The Body of Divinity Versifyed," in *The Man of God Furnished*, Boston, 1708. Evans, #1363, Jantz #25; and (D.) "The Body of Divinity *Versified*" in *The Way of Truth Laid Out*, Boston, 1721. Evans #2254, Jantz #25. *"The Body of Divinity Versified"* also appeared in Issac Watts's *Honey out of the Rock*, Boston, 1715, under the title *"The Body of Divinity Versify'd by Another Hand."* Evans #39639, Jantz #25; however, radical alterations of Mather's text by the compiler of that volume make collation of this version against those which Mather personally saw into print impossible. Another version of this verse, printed in this edition, see pp. 104–8, is also incorporated into Mather's "Instructions for children" in his *The A, B, C. of Religion*, Boston, 1713. Evans #1614, Jantz #46.

1. A God] A,C. A GOD
3. One] A. ONE
5. Our God,] A. indented
   known] A. Known
6. and] C,D. &
   Keeps, Rules] A. *Keeps, Rules*
7. To Glorify] A. indented
   God] A. GOD
8. men] D. Men
   me] D. Me
9. God] A. indented
   Rule] D. Rule
   Bible] A. Bible
10. Rule] C,D. *Rule*
    and] C,D. &
11. Holy] A. indented
    &] A,C,D. and
13. Tasting *Forbidden*] A. indented
14. all down to] C,D. *all down to*
15. Our Blest] A. indented
    in our Distress] C. *in our Distress;* D. *in our distress*

160

16. *to fetch*] A. to fetch
17. Into his] A. indented
    his] D. His
    Person] A. *Person*
    Son of God] A. Son of God
18. There] D. there
19. *Life* as] A. indented
    His People bring,] C. *His People bring*
20. &] A. and
21. For us] A. indented
    he] A,C.D. He
23. By Faith] A. indented
    Faith] A. Faith
    Christ] A. CHRIST
24. Faith] A. *Faith*
25. For *Sin*] A. indented
26. he'l] D. he'll
27. *Sinner's* receiving] A. indented;
29. All *Homage*] A. indented
    Homage] A. Homage
30. directed; A. Directed
    Heavenly Word] A. Heavenly Word
31. and] C,D. &
    Vain;] D. Vain
32. our *Work*] A. *our* Work
    Profane] A. profane
36. Get] A. get
37. &] A,D. and
    abhor] A. Abhor
39. Them who] A. indented
40. Gracious Covenant] A. *Gracious Covenant*
41. The *Baptism*] A. indented
    Baptism] A. Baptism
    Lord] A. Lord
43. To *See*] A. indented;
    Table] A. Table
    Sitt,] C. Sit,; D. Sit
44. Show] C. show,; D. show
45. *Gods Children*] A. indented
    Promises] A. Promises
    Enjoy:] D. Enjoy;
51. and] C,D. &
53. GOD,] D. GOD

"Conversion Exemplified."

Source: *Agreeable Admonitions for Old & Young*, Boston, 1703, pp. 43–48. Evans #1118, Jantz #28.

Collated against (A.) "The COVENANT Consented to," in *A Monitor for the Children of the Covenant*, Boston, 1715, p. 28 (fragment). Evans #39628, Jantz #28; (B.) "The Covenant Consented to," in *A Monitor for the Children of the Covenant*, 2d ed., Boston, 1725, pp. 28–30. Evans #39834; Jantz #28; and (C.)"The COVE-NANT Consented to," in *Baptismal Piety*, Boston, 1727, pp. 47–48. Evans #2907, Jantz #28. An untitled version of this poem, printed in this edition, also appeared in Mather's *Paterna*, pp. 175–77; see pp. 138–39 of Appendix A.

3. and] A. &
4. serve and please] A,B. *serve & please;* C. *serve, please*
6. *Wayes*] B,C. *Ways.*
   Soul] A,B,C. Soul
11. God] C. GOD
    alone:] A,B,C. *alone.*
14. Heaven] B,C. *Heaven*
    thus] A. I thus
    declare] A,B,C. *declare*
16. *Oh!*] A,B,C. *O!*
    Thou] C. *thou*
    Conquered Heart] A,B,C. *Conquered Heart*
19. Things] C. things;
21. Wilt] B,C. wilt
22. of a *Gods*] B. of *Gods;* C. *GOD's*
23. God] C. GOD
    Poor] A,B,C. *Poor*
24. sorts] A,B. Sorts
26. Conform] C. conform
29. Boundless] B,C. *Boundless*
    Wisdome] B. *Wisdom*
30. Boundless] B,C. *Boundless*
    ye] B. the
    Fruits] B,C. *Fruits*
    Give] B. give; C. give?
33. *Lord*] B,C. Lord
34. *Perfect*] C. *perfect*
    mind] B,C. Mind
35. *BLISS*] B. *Bliss*
    Word] C. Word,
41. God,] B,C. GOD,
42. forever] C. for ever
43. *Sight*] B,C. *Sight!*
44. Delight] B,C. *Delight*
47. !] B,C. I
48. and] B. &
50. and] B. &
51. God] C. GOD
52. *Will*] B,C. *will*
56. God] C. GOD
    my] C. *my*
58. *Judgment-Seat*] C. *Judgment Seat*
59. O] C. O
61. Pure] C. pure
    Scriptures-Way] *Scriptures way,*
62. Conduct] B. *Conduct;* C. conduct

162

63. Subdue] C. subdue
64. Renew.] C. Renew:
66. and] B. &
67. Possess] C. possess
    and] B. &
68. and, and] B. &, &
69. Sieze] C. sieze
70. alwayes] B,C. always
72. *He*] C. He

"My Satisfaction."

Source: *Meat out of the Eater,* Boston, 1703, p. 31. Evans #1127, Jantz #29.

"My Resignation."

Source: *Meat out of the Eater,* Boston, 1703, pp. 67–8. Evans #1127, Jantz #30. An earlier version, printed in this edition, also appeared in *Paterna,* pp. 137–38, under the title "Heb. 11. 17. with Gen. 22. 12;" see p. 137 of Appendix A.

"My Resolution."

Source: *Meat out of the Eater,* Boston, 1703, p. 108. Evans #1127, Jantz #31.

Collated against (A.) *Paterna,* p. 144, where it appears untitled in a section dated 1694; and (B.) "I stript of earthly, Comforts am," in Mather's *Diary,* 1695/6, 1:185–86. Jantz #7. See p. 137 of Appendix A. for the *Paterna* version.

1. Strip't] A. Stript B. stript
   Earthly] A. <u>Earthly</u> B. earthly,
   am:] A,B. am;
2. *Strip't*] A. *Stript* B. <u>Stript</u>
   let me] A. Lett me B. lett mee
   Mourn:] A,B. mourn:
3. *Naked*] A. <u>Naked</u>
   Earth] A. <u>Earth</u>
   came;] A,B. came,
4. *Naked*] A. <u>Naked</u> B. *naked*
   return] A. Return
5. *Gifts*] A. <u>Gifts</u>
   Above] A,B. above
   they?] A. They?
6. *gave*] A. <u>gave</u>
   me] A. mee
7. *Take*] A. <u>Take</u> B. *take*
   Flight] B. flight
8. *Taken*] A. <u>Taken</u>
   be] B. bee
10. For ever] A,B. Forever
    Adore:] A. Adore; B. adore;
11. *Wise*] A. <u>Wise</u> B. *wise*

Just] A. <u>Just</u> B. *just*
Sov'raign] A. <u>Sovereign</u> B. *soveraign*
still,] A. Still,

12. *Good* for ever more] A. <u>Good</u> forevermore.
    B. good forevermore.

"Songs in Such a Night."

Source: *Meat out of the Eater,* Boston, 1703, p. 142 (incorrectly numbered 124). Evans #1127, Jantz #32.

"My Text Paraphrased, and Faith Exhibited."

Source: *Meat out of the Eater,* Boston, 1703, pp. 181–82. Evans #1127, Jantz #33.

"Go then, my Dove"

Source: *Meat out of the Eater,* Boston, 1703, p. 186. Evans #1127, Jantz #34. Another version, printed in this edition, also appeared in Mather's *Diary,* November, 1702; see p. 140 of Appendix A.

"The Language of a Soul taken in,"

Source: "The Nets of Salvation" in *A Brief Essay, upon the Glorious Designs & Methods Of Winning the Minds of Men unto Serious Religion,* Boston, 1704, pp. 55–56. Evans #1176.

"The Consent."

Source: *Parental Wishes and Charges,* Boston, 1705, pp. 58–60. Evans #1219.

"A Poem Dedicated to the Memory of the Reverend and Excellent Mr. Urian Oakes"

Source: Boston, 1682. Evans #319, Jantz #1.

142. here)] originally "here"
212. fear'd] originally "fea'rd"
392. sight.] originally "sight"

"An Elegy on The Death of . . . The Reverend Mr. Nathanael Collins"

Source: "An Elegy On The Much-to-be-deplored Death of That Never-to-be-forgotten Person, The Reverend Mr. Nathanael Collins," Boston, 1685 (p. 17 is omitted by number in the original). Evans #392, Jantz #2.

Title: COLLINS,] originally "COLLINS?"

165: spar'd] originally "spar d"
254. giv'n] originally "giv,n"

287. wo.] originally "wo"
359. plac't] originally "plac,t"

"An Elegy Upon the Death of Mrs. Mary Brown;"

Source: *Eureka. The Vertuous Woman found*, Boston, 1704, pp. 1–8. Evans #1121.

102. *Death*] originally *"Daath"*
164. *New.*] originally *"New"*

"A Lacrymatory; Design'd for the Tears let fall at the Funeral of Mrs. Sarah Leveret"

Source: *Monica Americana*, Boston, 1705, pp. 29–32. Evans #1217, Jantz #35.

92. withold.] originally "withold"
106. flew.] originally "flew"

"On the Graves, of My Young Brethren"

Source: *Vigilantius*, Boston, 1706, pp. 29–34. Evans #1265, Jantz #38.

Title. Brackets are Mather's

63. *Proud*] originally *"Pround"*
160. *Oblivions*] originally *"Oblivjons"*

"Gratitudinis Ergo. An Essay on the Memory of my Venerable Master, Ezekiel Cheever."

Source: *Corderius Americanus*, Boston, 1708, pp. 26–34. Evans #1361, Jantz #40.

82. Then] originally "the"
114. Thought,] originally "Thought."

"Epitaph" (on Shubael Dummer)

Source: *Fair Weather*, Boston, 1691, pp. 92–93. Evans #560, Jantz #4.

Collated against (A.) "Epitaph," in *Decennium Luctuosum*, Boston, 1699. Evans #873, Jantz #4; and (B.) *Magnalia Christi Americana*, Vol. 2, London, 1702, p. 531. Jantz #4. (A.) and (B.) are 16-line abridged versions.

1. *Shephard*] A,B. *Shepherd*
   Sacrific'd] A. Sacrific'd,
2. Priz'd;] A,B. priz'd.
3. Churches] A. *Churches*
   Light,] B. *Light,*
4. Heaven] A,B. *Heav'n*
   Hell] A,B. *Hell*
   Spite.] A. *Spite:* B. *Spight.*

5. Countreyes] A. Countrys B. Countries
      Face] A. *Face,*
   6. *Knew*] A,B. knew
      Grace] A,B. *Grace*
   7. line eliminated in A. and B.
   8. line eliminated in A. and B.
   9. *Divels*] A,B. *Devils*
  10. Reciev'd] A,B. Receiv'd
  11. Bled,] A,B. Bled
  12. Leave] A,B. leave
      the Saints] A,B. his Charge
      Unfed] A,B. Unfed
  13. DUMMER, the] A,B. A Proper
  14. *Shot*] A,B. Shot
      Flown] A. Flow'n B. Flown
      trice;] A,B. Trice.
  15. line eliminated in A. and B.
  16. line eliminated in A. and B.
  17. line eliminated in A. and B.
  18. line eliminated in A. and B.
  19. LORD] A,B. Lord
      Cry of Righteous] A,B. Cry of *Righteous*
      DUMMERS Wounds,] A. Dummers wounds B. DUMMER'S
      Wounds.
  20. Under thine *Altar;* Lord, Rate off those *Hounds*]
      A,B. Ascending still against the *Salvage Hounds,*
  21. thus thy *Flocks:*] A,B. thy dear *Flocks;*
      And let the *Bones*] A,B. and let the *Cry*
  22. line eliminated in A. and B.
  23. line eliminated in A. and B.
  24. line eliminated in A. and B.
      [Replaced with] A. Add Force to *Theirs,* that at
      thine *Altar* ly. B. Add Force to *Theirs* that at
      thine *Altar* lye.

"The Excellent Wigglesworth, Remembred by some Good Tokens."

Source: *A Faithful Man, Described and Rewarded*, Boston, 1705, p. 48. Evans #1212, Jantz #36.

"Little Children Brought unto the Lord Jesus Christ."

Source: From Mather's Appendix, "A Token, for the Children of New-England," added as a supplement to James Janeway's *A Token for Children*, Boston, 1700, pp. 29–30. Evans #914, Jantz #17 (misprinted 16).

"Early Religion."

Source: "A Token, for the Children of New-England," Boston, 1700, pp. 30–31. Evans #914, Jantz #18.

"Psal. 119.9."

3. Call'd] originally "Call d"

"The Consent of the Believer unto the Ten Commandments."

Source: "A Token, for the Children of New-England," Boston, 1700, pp. 31–32.
Evans #914, Jantz #19.

"The Lords Prayer."

Source: "A Token, for the Children of New-England," Boston, 1700, pp. 32–34.
Evans #914, Jantz #20.

Collated against "The Lords Prayer," in *Maschil, Or, the Faithful Instructor,* Boston,
1702, p. 189. Evans #1069, Jantz #26.

5. Ever-glorious] Ever glorious
6. Adore:] Adore;
7. All] all;
   same,] same
9. Pray] Pray;
10. *the*] the
12. *the*] the
27. Let] let

"The Lords-Day."

Source: "A Token, for the Children of New-England," Boston, 1700, pp. 34–35.
Evans #914, Jantz #21.

"Prayer Encouraged"

Source: "A Token, for the Children of New-England," Boston, 1700, pp. 35-36.
Evans #914, Jantz #22.

"Instructions for Children."

Source: *The A, B, C. of Religion,* Boston, 1713, pp. 37–42. Evans #1614, Jantz #46.

"The Body of Divinity Versifyed."

18. *Live.*] originally *"Live"*
22. Frame.] originally "Frame"

"Singing at the Plow."

Source: "The Plain Songs of the Pious Husbandman; In the Work of his Husban-
dry, and the House of his Pilgrimmage," in *Agricola. Or, the Religious
Husbandman,* Boston, 1727, p. 21. Evans #2905, Jantz #51.

"The Sower a Singer."

Source: "The Plain Songs . . ." in *Agricola*, Boston, 1727, pp. 96–97. Evans #2905, Jantz #52.

"The Rain gasped for."

Source: "The Plain Songs . . ." in *Agricola*, Boston, 1727, p. 131. Evans #2905, Jantz #53.

"The Song of the Sithe."

Source: "The Plain Songs . . ." in *Agricola*, Boston, 1727, pp. 151–52. Evans #2905, Jantz #54.

    5. *God!*] originally "*GOD*"

"The Songs of God, Singing among the Trees of God;"

Source: "The Plain Songs . . ." in *Agricola*, Boston, 1727, pp. 190–91. Evans #2905, Jantz #55.

"The Songs of Harvest."

Source: "The Plain Songs . . ." in *Agricola*, Boston, 1727, p. 212. Evans #2905, Jantz #56.

    5. *I've*] originally "*Iv'e*"

["The Mercies of Almighty God"]

Source: *The Christian Thank-Offering*, Boston, 1696, p. 32. Evans #752, Jantz #9.

["Isaiah XXVI."]

Source: *Appendix to the Psalms, Hymns and Spiritual Songs of the Old and New Testaments: Faithfully Translated into English Meetre*, 10th ed., Boston, 1702. Evans #1039, Jantz #12.

"The Song of the Pardoned."

Source: "Divine Hymns" in *The Everlasting Gospel*, Boston, 1700, p. 74. Evans #923, Jantz #13.

"Good Inferences."

Source: "Divine Hymns" in *The Everlasting Gospel*, Boston, 1700, p. 75. Evans #923, Jantz #14.

"The Lessons of the Gospel."

Source: "Divine Hymns" in *The Everlasting Gospel*, Boston, 1700, pp. 75–76. Evans #923, Jantz #15.

15. through] originally "thorough"

"Evening Thoughts."

Source: "Divine Hymns" in *The Everlasting Gospel*, Boston, 1700, p. 76. Evans #923, Jantz #16.

Collated against (A.) "Phil. 1. 21." in *Paterna*, p. 65; and (B.) "Phil. 1. 21." in the *Diary*, September, 1683, 1:75–76.

1. *Life:*] A. <u>Life</u>; B. Life;
2. *Enliven'd Faith.*] A. Enliven'd <u>Faith.</u>
   B. *enlivened Faith*
3. now] A. <u>Now</u> B. *now*
   'twill] A. *t'will* B. twill
   Gain] A. <u>Gain</u>
   Dy,] A. <u>Dy,</u> B. dy
4. fetch'd] A. fetcht
   Stingless Death] A. <u>Stingless Death</u>
   B. *Stingless Death*

"An Hymn. The Right Understanding of much Affliction."

Source: *A Companion for the Afflicted*, Boston, 1701, p. 56. Evans #992, Jantz #23.

"Tried, and Coming forth as Gold."

Source: A Soul Well-Anchored, Boston, 1721, title page. Evans #1558, Jantz #44.

Title, Stanza 4] terminal punctuation added after "GOD"

"X. Commandments."

Source: *A Spiritual Catechism*, Boston, 1691, title page. Evans #565, Jantz #3.

"The Ten Commandments."

Source: *Maschil, Or, The Faithful Instructor*, Boston, 1702, p. 188. Evans #1069, Jantz #3.

"A Preparatory Thanksgiving-Song, fetch'd from the Beginning and Conclusion of the Hundred and Third Psalm."

Source: *The Christian Thank-Offering*, Boston, 1696, title page. Evans #752, Jantz #8.

"High Attainments."

Source: *Diary*, May, 1683, 1:59.

[Hymn.]

Source: *Diary*, October, 1683, 1:75–76.

Collated against *Paterna*, p. 65, where it appears untitled in a section dated 1683. The last stanza of this verse was also published separately under the title "Evening Thoughts," in *The Everlasting Gospel*, Boston, 1700, p. 76. Evans #923, Jantz #16; see p. 125 and p. 169 of this section.

1. Blest] I. Blest
   bee] be
   JEHOVAH] JEHOVAH,
2. mee] me
   Daily Blessings Load] <u>Daily Blessings</u> Load.
3. Saviour] <u>Saviour</u>
   Bestow] bestow
4. *Salvations* on mee] <u>Salvations</u> on me
5. To Thee] II. To Thee
   Wayes] <u>Wayes</u>
6. Words] <u>Words</u>
7. Thoughts;] <u>Thoughts</u>:
   Faults] <u>Faults</u>
   own;] own:
8. all] All
   Christ] CHRIST
   pardon'd] <u>Pardon'd</u>
9. Thy] III. Thy
   Life] <u>Life</u>
10. *enlivened Faith*] Enliven'd <u>Faith</u>
11. *now* twill bee my *Gain* to dy] <u>Now</u> t'wil be my
    <u>Gain</u> to <u>Dy</u>,
12. fetcht] fetch'd
    stingless Death] <u>Stingless Death</u>

"Health, Bread, with Life, my God mee sends"

Source: *Diary*, Winter, 1692, 1:154. Jantz #5.

"Lord, bought by thy All-worthy Blood"

Source: *Diary*, Winter, 1692, 1:155. Jantz #6.

Collated against *Paterna*, pp. 65–66, where it appears untitled in a section dated 1683.

1. Lord] <u>Lord</u>
   bought] Bought

Blood] Blood
2. *Life, worthless I Receive:*] Life Worthless I
receive:
3. *Health, and Peace, and Food,*] Health, & Peace,
& Food,
4. *Plagues, I live.*] plagues I Live.
5. From thy *great Friendship*] By Thy great
Friendship
6. *Friends*] Friends
Jewels] Jewels
7. Mee Thou dost in thy *Church* employ] Mee in thy
Work, thou dost Employ:
8. still] Still
Prayer.] Prayer.
9. His *Promise*] with His Promises
mine;] Mine,
10. Angels] *Angels*
Guard.] Guard;
11. I'l my long *Praises* therefore join,] Now I will
my Long Praises join
12. With Thy good *Angels, Lord.*] With thy Good
Angels, LORD.

["In Peace with God Ly down I Will."]

Source: *Paterna,* section dated 1685, p. 95.

"Heb. 11. 17 with Gen. 22. 12"

Source: *Paterna,* section dated 1694, pp. 137–38. This verse also appeared under the title "My Resignation" in *Meat out of the Eater,* Boston, 1703, p. 31. Evans #1127, Jantz #30; in this edition, see p. 41.

["I Stript of Earthly Comforts . . ."]

Source: *Paterna,* section dated 1694, p. 144. This verse also appeared under the title "My Resolution" in *Meat out of the Eater,* Boston, 1703, p. 108. Evans #1127, Jantz #31; in this edition, see p. 42. Another version also appeared in the *Diary,* February, 1695/6. p. 185. See notes for text from *Meat out of the Eater,* p. 163, for collation of all versions.

["And now to Life Rais'd by the Heavenly . . ."]

Source: *Paterna,* section dated 1697, p. 175. Other versions of this verse are collated in notes on "Conversion Exemplified" (from Mather's *Agreeable Admonitions for Old & Young,* Boston, 1703); see pp. 161–63 for complete collation.

["I did lift up my Voice to Jah,"]

Source: *Diary,* June, 1702, 1:431.

["Go then, my DOVE"]

Source: *Diary,* November, 1702, 1:450. Another version, included in this edition, also appeared in *Meat out of the Eater,* Boston, 1703, p. 186; see p. 44.

"The Sons of God shouting for Joy at the Arrival of the Lord's-day."

Source: *Diary,* December, 1711, 2:138.

["O Glorious Christ of God; I live"]

Source: *Diary,* February, 1724/25, 2:786.

["On my dear Liza I this Book bestow . . ."]

Source: [Hand-inscribed in] *Coelestinus. A Conversation in Heaven, Quickened and Assisted, with Discoveries of Things in the Heavenly World,* Boston, 1723. The original copy bearing the inscription is in the Elkins Collection of the Philadelphia Free Library.

"The Pidgeon Py. A Poem in Imitation of the Monumental Gratitude."

Source: [Hand-inscribed in] John Hubbard, *A Monumental Gratitude,* New London, 1727. Jantz #59. The original copy is in private possession; a facsimile appears in *Photostat Americana,* Boston, 1925, 139: n. pag.

Select Bibliography

Bercovitch, Sacvan. *Typology and Early American Literature.* [Amherst]: University of Massachusetts Press, 1972.

Boas, Ralph and Louise. *Cotton Mather: Keeper of the Puritan Conscience.* Hamden, Conn.: Archon Books, 1964.

Bradstreet, Anne. *The Works of Anne Bradstreet.* Ed. Jeannine Hensley. Cambridge: Harvard University Press, Belknap Press, 1967.

Bristol, Roger. *Supplement to Charles Evans' American Bibliography.* Charlottesville: University Press of Virginia, 1970.

Cohen, Hennig. "A Cotton Mather Verse Inscription." *American Notes and Queries* 1 (December 1962): 53–54.

Daly, Robert. *God's Altar: The World and Flesh in Puritan Poetry.* Berkeley and Los Angeles: University of California Press, 1978.

Evans, Charles. *The American Bibliography: A Chronological Dictionary of all Books, Pamphlets and Periodical Publications in the USA, 1639–1800.* 14 vols. New York: Peter Smith, 1941.

Holmes, Thomas J. *Cotton Mather: A Bibliography of His Works.* 3 vols. Cambridge: Massachusetts Historical Society, 1940.

Jantz, Harold S. *The First Century of New England Verse.* New York: Russell and Russell, 1943.

Levin, David. *Cotton Mather, The Young Life of the Lord's Remembrancer, 1663–1703.* Cambridge: Harvard University Press, 1978.

Lowance, Mason I. "Typology and the New England Way: Cotton Mather and the Exegesis of Biblical Types." *Early American Literature* 4, no. 1 (1969): 15–37.

Mannierre, William R. "Cotton Mather and the Biographical Parallel." *American Quarterly* 13 (Spring 1961): 153–60.

Mather, Cotton. *The Diary of Cotton Mather.* Ed. Worthington Chauncey Ford. 2 vols. New York, n.d.

———. "Biblia Americana." Unpublished manuscript. Boston: Massachusetts Historical Society.

———. *Magnalia Christi Americana.* Ed. Thomas Robbins. 2 vols. Hartford, 1852.

———. *Manuductio ad Ministerium.* Vol. 2, *The Puritans: A Sourcebook of Their Writings.* Ed. Perry Miller and Thomas H. Johnson. New York: Harper and Row, 1963.

———. *Paterna.* Ed. Ronald A. Bosco. Delmar, N.Y.: Scholars' Facsimiles and Reprints, 1976.

173

Mather, Richard. Preface to the *Bay Psalm Book*. Vol. 2, *The Puritans: A Sourcebook of Their Writings*. Ed. Perry Miller and Thomas H. Johnson. New York: Harper and Row, 1963.

Meserole, Harrison T. *Seventeenth-Century American Poetry*. New York: New York University Press, 1968.

Miller, Perry and Johnson, Thomas H. *The Puritans: A Sourcebook of Their Writings*. Vol. 2. New York: Harper and Row, 1963.

Murdock, Kenneth B. *Handkerchiefs from Paul*. Cambridge: Harvard University Press, 1927.

———. *Literature and Theology in Colonial New England*. Cambridge: Harvard University Press, 1949.

Salska, Agnieszka. "Puritan Poetry: Its Public and Private Strain." *Early American Literature* 19 (1984): 107–21.

Silverman, Kenneth. *Colonial American Poetry*. New York: Hafner, 1968.

———. *The Selected Letters of Cotton Mather*. Baton Rouge: Louisiana State University Press, 1971.

———. *The Life and Times of Cotton Mather*. New York: Harper and Row, 1984.

Wendell, Barrett. *Cotton Mather: The Puritan Priest*. New York: Dodd, Mead, 1891.